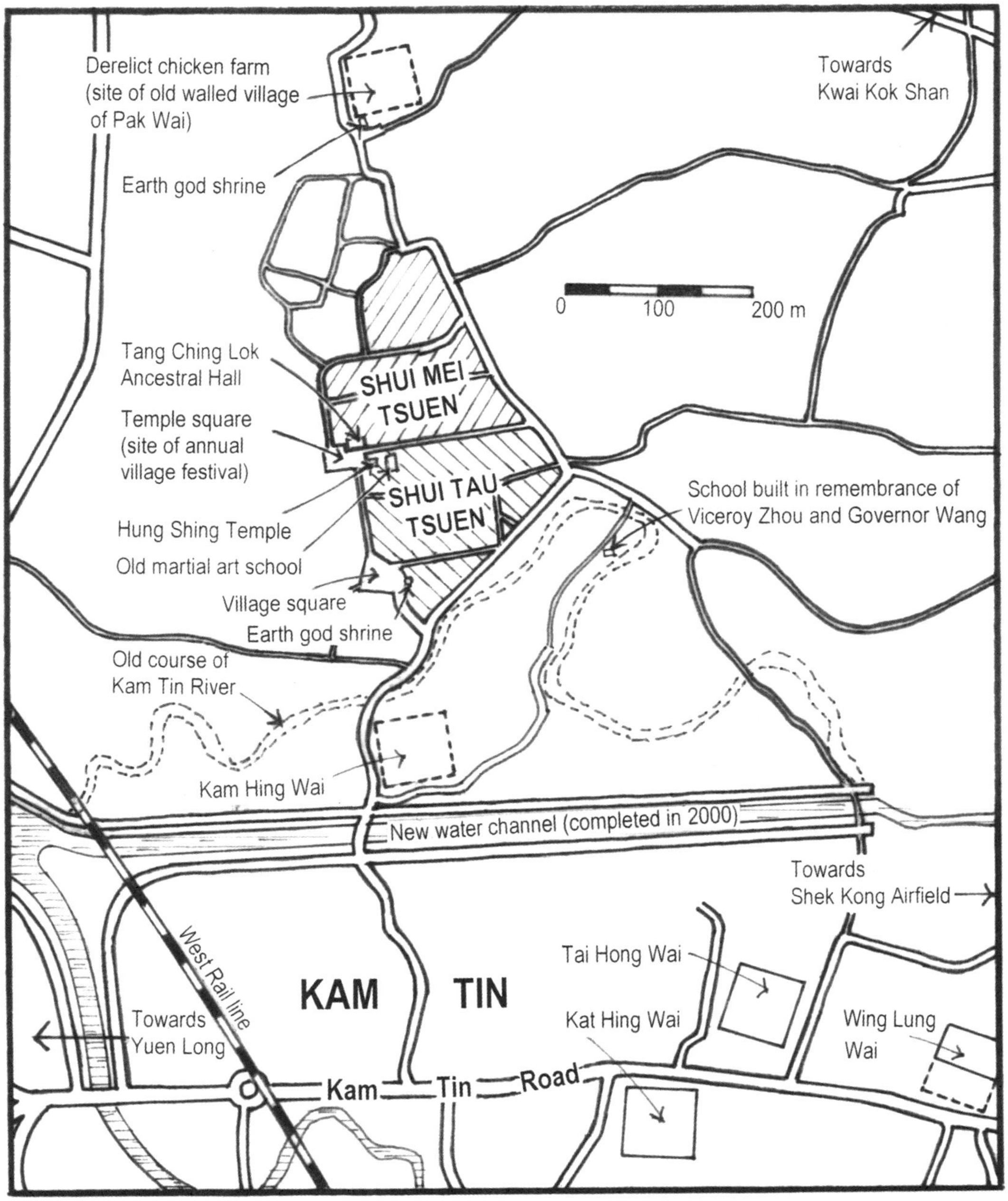

Derelict chicken farm (site of old walled village of Pak Wai)
Towards Kwai Kok Shan
Earth god shrine
0
100
200 m
Tang Ching Lok Ancestral Hall
SHUI MEI TSUEN
Temple square (site of annual village festival)
SHUI TAU TSUEN
Hung Shing Temple
Old martial art school
Village square
Earth god shrine
School built in remembrance of Viceroy Zhou and Governor Wang
Old course of Kam Tin River
Kam Hing Wai
New water channel (completed in 2000)
Towards Shek Kong Airfield
West Rail line
KAM TIN
Tai Hong Wai
Towards Yuen Long
Kat Hing Wai
Wing Lung Wai
Kam Tin Road

A Tale of Two Villages
The Story of Changing Village Life in the New Territories

Fig. 1 Chou Wong Yi Kung Study Shue Yuen, the traditional school built in 1685 in Shui Tau Tsuen in honour of Viceroy Zhou and Governor Wang, who were responsible for persuading the emperor to end the draconian Coastal Evacuation Order. Even though the building no longer functions as a school today, it remains a memorial to that tragic event in which many villagers perished. *(Lee Ho Yin)*

A Tale of Two Villages
The Story of Changing Village Life in the New Territories

Lee Ho Yin and **Lynne D. DiStefano**

OXFORD
UNIVERSITY PRESS

OXFORD
UNIVERSITY PRESS

Oxford University Press is a department of the University of Oxford.
It furthers the University's objective of excellence in research, scholarship,
and education by publishing worldwide in

Oxford New York

Auckland Bangkok Buenos Aires Cape Town Chennai
Dar es Salaam Delhi Hong Kong Istanbul Karachi Kolkata
Kuala Lumpur Madrid Melbourne Mexico City Mumbai Nairobi
São Paulo Shanghai Taipei Tokyo Toronto

Oxford is a registered trade mark of Oxford University Press

Published in the United States
by Oxford University Press Inc., New York

© Oxford University Press 2002

First published in 2002

This impression (lowest digit)
1 3 5 7 9 10 8 6 4 2

All rights reserved. No part of this publication may be reproduced,
stored in a retrieval system, or transmitted, in any form or by any means,
without the prior permission in writing of Oxford University Press,
or as expressly permitted by Law, or under terms agreed with the appropriate
reprographics rights organization. Enquiries concerning reproduction
outside the scope of the above should be sent to the Rights Department,
Oxford University Press, at the address below
You must not circulate this book in any other binding or cover
and you must impose the same condition on any acquirer

British Library Cataloguing in Publication Data
available

Library of Congress Cataloging-in-Publication-Data
available

ISBN 0-19-592859-8

Printed in Hong Kong
Published by Oxford University Press (China) Ltd
18th Floor, Warwick House East, Taikoo Place, 979 King's Road, Quarry Bay
Hong Kong

For **Tang Tim-kau,** and
the people of **Water Head Village** and **Water Tail Village**

Contents

Acknowledgements   **9**
    Notes on Romanization   **11**
        Preface   **13**
            Introduction   **19**

Chapter 1
Enter the Tang Clan: History of Kam Tin until the Late 19th Century   25

- Beyond the Villages: Kam Tin in Context
- Genesis: The Founding of Kam Tin
- Pak Wai and Nam Wai: The Tangs' First Villages
- Accidental Royalty: The Tang who Married a Lost Princess
- Wong Ku: Life and Death of a Princess
- Fields of Splendour: The Naming of Kam Tin
- War and Peace: The Impact of Dynastic Transition
- Aftermath: Changing Demography and Habitat in Post-evacuation Kam Tin

Chapter 2
The British are Coming: The Union Jack over Kam Tin   61

- Barbarians at the Gate: The British Arrive in Kam Tin
- Rebel without a Cause: The Battle of Kam Tin
- Conciliation: Relations between the Tangs and the British during the Colonial Period

Chapter 3
Recent Past: Kam Tin after World War II　　79

- From Farmland to Real Estate: The Decline of Agriculture in the New Territories
- The Small House Policy: The Shape of Villages to Come
- Breaking the Political Monopoly: Women's Rights and Voting Rights of Non-indigenous Villagers
- Hung Shing and Ding Dung: The Persistence of Village Cultural Traditions
- The End of Village Tradition: The Future of Shui Tau Tsuen and Shui Mei Tsuen

Chapter 4
Village Voice: The World According to the Tangs　　109

- Traditional Past to Modern Present
- The Young Village Representative's Story
- The Rice Farmer's Story
- The Old Village Chief's Story

Bibliography　　**129**

　　Index　　**133**

　　　　About the Authors　　**135**

Acknowledgements

IT IS AN UNDERSTATEMENT TO SAY that the research for this book has been a painstaking task. Since the two villages have never before been written about in the kind of detail attempted in this book, the authors had to search for information literally from the ground up. Over a period of four years, we spent a great deal of time visiting the villages, talking to the inhabitants, and making photographic records of scenes and events. It was hard work, but would have been much harder had it not been for the support of villagers, friends, and colleagues. We would like to take this opportunity to thank them.

To the many kind villagers of Shui Tau Tsuen and Shui Mei Tsuen, thank you for opening your hearts to us, and for treating us like good friends rather than the inquisitive strangers we really were. In particular, to Tang Tim-kau, his son Johnny Tang, and their families and relatives, we cannot thank you enough for sharing your stories and inviting us to your family and community gatherings. Without your kindness and generosity, the research for this book would have been impossible.

To the editors and staff members of Oxford University Press—in particular Rebecca Ng for her initial support of this book, Anastasia Edwards for managing the project, Barbara Baker for editing the manuscript, and Karen Szeto for administering the project—thank you for taking an interest in our book proposal and pursuing it with patience and persistence. Without you, there would certainly be no book and the stories of the villages would be lost to future generations.

Thanks are also due to our friends and colleagues at The University of Hong Kong, without whose constant support and encouragement we might have taken the easy path and put off completing this book. Thank you Professor Richard Frewer and wife Carolyn, who never failed to ask about our book and urged us to complete it at the soonest date. Thank you Professor David Lung for inspiring us to take an active interest in Hong Kong's cultural heritage and for sharing valuable insights. Thank you Carol Lai for your patient assistance during photographic trips to the villages, and for being so prompt with our imaging and printing needs. Thank you Rosemary Tan for helping us in seemingly little ways that actually meant a great deal to us.

We would also like to acknowledge the contributions of the following people: staff members of the University of Hong Kong's Main Library; Bernard Hui and his colleagues at the Government Records Service, Public Records Office; L. Y. Kwok and his colleagues at the Photographic Library, Information Services Department. You have no idea how much your excellent services have helped us in our research. In addition we would like to thank the University of Hong Kong's Committee on Research and Conference Grant for funding the research for this book.

To Brian Lam, Josephine Wong, and their colleagues at the Hong Kong Museum of History, thank you for being so prompt and helpful when we needed quick answers to urgent questions. Thank you also Sharif Shams Imon, Tim Ko, and Jason Wordie, for your research help. Without all of you, the difficult task of research for this book would have been even more difficult. Thank you Dr. Yvonne Archibald, for helping to proofread the final text.

Our thanks also go to members of John Leung Studios Ltd., particularly, Sinia Leung, John Leung, Veronica Chan, Gloria Leung, and Paul Tam, who have been most helpful in accommodating our photographic requirements. Your professionalism and friendliness towards customers are what make Hong Kong such a wonderful place to be.

To Professor Joseph DiStefano, a very special thanks for letting the authors hole up in your quiet Swiss chalet apartment for the summer of 2001, so that we could concentrate on finishing the manuscript. In a strange way, it was fitting that this book, about two historical Chinese villages in Hong Kong, jointly written by a Chinese and a Westerner, was put together in an historical village in Switzerland.

Notes on Romanization

ONE OF THE COMPLICATIONS ENCOUNTERED by the authors in writing this book is the confusion between the different official systems of Romanization of the Chinese language used in Hong Kong and mainland China. The Hong Kong Government adopts the Eitel/Dyer–Ball system of Romanization, which is based on the spoken Cantonese language. On the other hand, the mainland Chinese authorities have standardized the Romanization of Chinese names and places using the Putonghua (Mandarin) based Pinyin system. The Pinyin system, properly known as Hanyu Pinyin ('Chinese language phonetic transliteration'), was first introduced by the Government of the People's Republic of China in 1958. In 1979, the Pinyin system was officially enforced to supersede old Romanization systems such as the once common Wade–Giles system. It would be convenient to standardize the Romanization of names and places mentioned in this book in Pinyin. In reality, such expediency would not only be impractical, but also confusing, since names within Hong Kong would be rendered totally unrecognizable. For example, the familiar local names of Kam Tin and Tang would become the unfamiliar Jintian and Deng. Hence, to retain cognitive integrity, those names and terminologies that directly apply to Hong Kong will retain their Cantonese-based Romanization, but cross-referencing with the Pinyin system will be included, when appropriate, in italics within parentheses.

Preface

I REMEMBER PRECISELY WHEN MY FASCINATION with people of traditional cultures and their living environment began. It was some twenty years ago, when I was sent to Borneo for jungle warfare training as part of my military service. One day, at the fringe of the jungle in the middle of nowhere, waiting for the helicopter ferry that seemed to take forever to come, I decided to wander around to take my mind off the sweltering heat and the swarm of mosquitoes hovering around my face. A knocking sound caught my attention and I followed it to a clearing in the jungle, where the scene that appeared before my eyes amazed me. An old tribal man, wearing nothing but a loincloth and carrying a long machete on his back, was busy hacking a log with a small hand axe. Behind him was the incomplete end of an enormous longhouse. The old man was extending the building that housed his entire village all by himself!

Several topless women and naked children appeared high on the stilted platform at the open end of the longhouse and stared suspiciously at this curious stranger in green camouflage uniform, who was carrying a menacing-looking rifle. The old man stopped momentarily from his chore and looked up. I smiled and waved my hand to show that I was friendly, and, with a slight nod, he continued his work while I continued to watch and wonder with increasing curiosity. But with the faint whooping sound of the approaching helicopter, I had to return to the landing zone to join my teammates. This was my first contact with a living community that was totally different from the one I was brought up in and familiar with. Who were those people? What was their history, and what were their traditions, customs, beliefs, and practices? How long could they maintain their traditional way of life before they succumbed to the trappings of a modern lifestyle? Questions whirled in my head as the helicopter raced above the dense canopy of the tropical rainforest, and these were the same questions whirling in my head some fifteen years later when I began working on a book about another traditional village community with a friend.

In mid 1997, I met Lynne DiStefano, the co-author of this book, at the University of Hong Kong, and we soon became good friends and close colleagues. By then my interest in traditional village culture and architecture had spurred me to take up doctoral studies on the subject. While studying at the University of Hong Kong, I had the opportunity to indulge myself with frequent visits to remote places in the New Territories to look at traditional villages. I offered to take Lynne to visit my favourite local village, and she, having just arrived in Hong Kong, accepted my offer out of a mixture of boredom and curiosity. Coming from the Canadian province of Ontario, where picturesque villages of cottages surrounded by open fields constitute the rural landscape, Lynne inevitably conjured a similar mental picture of the 'rural' New Territories. As we arrived at the fringe of the village after a short mini-bus ride from the town of Yuen Long, she asked, 'So, where is this favourite village of yours that you've been talking so much about?' 'You're standing right in it,' I replied. She was surprised, as she did not expect to see so much concrete, so little greenery, and virtually no farmland, and, most of all, to be greeted by a green-tiled concrete public toilet at the entrance to the village proper. Perhaps I should have explained to her the differences between what is understood as 'rural' in Hong Kong and in Ontario. Like many other long-time residents of Hong Kong, I had come to take for granted the semi-urbanized 'rural' landscape of the New Territories, where three-storey modern concrete village houses, incongruously known as 'Spanish villas', are interspersed with their traditional single-storey, grey-brick predecessors.

The village in question is actually two archetypal non-walled villages found in an area called Kam Tim in the New Territories: Shui Tau Tsuen (literally 'Water Head Village') and Shui Mei Tsuen ('Water Tail Village'). Like a pair of conjoined twins, the villages are physically connected and it is hard to tell where the separating boundary lies. Located some distance from the main road and not well known to tourists and local urbanites, the villages attract few curious visitors. Yet these two villages stand apart because of their relatively intact village pattern and a number of surviving traditional village buildings—study halls, ancestral halls, temples, and houses. And associated with these buildings are nine hundred years of history as well as age-old but active traditions, customs, and beliefs, unique to Hong Kong's traditional clan-based villages.

As we explored, we came upon a row of traditional houses that I had not noticed before. We poked our heads into an opened door and saw a stove, built with brick and fired by wood, with an enormous wok sitting on it (in Hong Kong's traditional village houses, the cooking area is located at the front of the house). A woman came out and stared with hostility at my camera hanging against my chest, and, knowing how camera-shy the local villagers were, I started apologizing and was about to beat a hasty retreat. As I stepped away from the doorway, the woman noticed the Caucasian woman standing behind me, and the surprise caused her to break into an involuntarily giggle. Seizing the opportunity, I quickly explained that my 'professor' had never seen a more attractive house than hers and would like to look at it. That did the trick, as education and scholarly achievement have always been highly valued in Hong Kong's traditional village society. With the knowledge that we were from a prestigious local university, she relaxed and started talking to us. We, or more correctly, Lynne, the honourable professor, was introduced to her father, the then elected village chief of Shui Mei Tsuen. That was the beginning of our formal relationship with the family of the village patriarch.

As I explained to Lynne later, villagers in the New Territories often showed more friendliness to Westerners than to local Chinese, as they considered the former to be more sensitive and respectful of the things they valued most—their traditional customs, beliefs, and practices. The following year, when we returned to attend the annual village festival with Barbara Baker, the editor of this book, who was living in Hong Kong at the time, I suffered the unpleasant experience of incurring the wrath of a local woman for taking her picture without permission. In a lapse of good judgment, I raised my camera at an elderly woman dressed in splendid traditional costume and pressed the shutter release, thinking that her lack of protest in having my camera aimed at her was sufficient consent to take her picture. As soon as she heard the click of my camera, she came charging at me, nose flaring and screaming at the top of her voice. Her young son, in defence of his mother's dignity, soon came running to join in the fray. Lynne and Barbara were shocked by the ferocity of the woman's reaction, and, unsure what to do, quietly slipped away, leaving me to exercise my wits and diplomacy. Thanks to a couple of friendly villagers who intervened, my apology was reluctantly accepted, with a promise that I would return the offending negative. Hence, when we carried out field research on the villages for this book, Lynne, the respected professor and sensitive Westerner, became very much the key that unlocked the hearts and minds of villagers, giving us access to homes, stories, and photographs.

As we left the villages on Lynne's first visit, we felt reassuringly safe that they would not be caught in the development frenzy that was happening elsewhere in Hong Kong. At least, we hoped, not in the foreseeable future. Little did we know that in a few months' time, in November 1997 to be exact, the Kowloon–Canton Railway Corporation (KCRC) would announce the West Rail Project, a mega infrastructure-building programme that would be the prelude to massive urbanization plans for many areas in the western part of the New Territories, including the area in which our favourite villages are located. It was heartbreaking news for us when we learned of the West Rail Project and its implication for the villages. That was when Lynne suggested that we should write a book about Shui Tau and Shui Mei as we knew them, before they faded away from their present form and from the collective memory of the people of Hong Kong.

Although Lynne is clearly not Chinese, we have decided to write the book in the first person plural, as if we were of the same Chinese origin. In a way, this has become the case, as the villagers have come to accept Lynne as though she were a familiar Chinese friend. At times, it was amusing to see them speaking and laughing together (with me as an unnoticed interpreter!), in total oblivion to the fact that they did not share the same ethnicity or speak the same language.

Lee Ho Yin
June 2002, Hong Kong

Introduction

ON 1 JULY 1997, Hong Kong ceased to be a British colony, and it became an autonomous Special Administrative Region under Chinese sovereignty. Among the challenges now faced by Hong Kong is that of finding an identity that can truly represent post-colonial Hong Kong. Poor Hong Kong has always been a confused child, as its cultural identity has always been slightly obscured by the issue of nationality. Many of us were once both Chinese people and British subjects. Now we are not quite Chinese citizens, but Hong Kong Residents holding passports issued by a host of regional and national governments, including Hong Kong, Britain, Canada, and Singapore. Since we cannot find a clear-cut correlation between our identity and nationality, we have to look elsewhere. In our desperate search for an identity, we seem willing to cling onto anything with which we think we can identify ourselves. As a result, our identity becomes relegated to a hodgepodge of symbols that range from the literary Confucius to the martial Bruce Lee, from the non-existent Chinese junk to the obsolescent cross-harbour ferry, and from the mythical dragon to the endangered pink dolphin. We seem to have forgotten that cultural identity is not a trademark that can be printed on a T-shirt. Rather, it is the intangible essence of the local people that can only be discovered from within their past and present—of who they are and where they come from.

It is no simple matter to try to trace the roots of the Hong Kong people, as the vast majority of local people had not settled in the territory until two or three generations ago. However, there is one place in Hong Kong where a part of the population has been settled for centuries, and in some places, perhaps close to a millennium. This is the New Territories, the now semi-urbanized 'rural' part of Hong Kong, which has always been a part of China except for a brief period of ninety-nine years (1898 to 1997), during which it was only temporarily leased to Britain. The people that belong to this land are the so-called 'indigenous villagers' who are able to trace their ancestry to a time that we can only begin to imagine, largely based on what is presented or misrepresented in books, operas, movies, and television. Arguably, these villagers are more representative of the roots of the Hong Kong people than anyone. This view is strengthened by the fact that the lineages of the vast majority of Hong Kong people are not dissimilar to those of the indigenous villagers, whose genealogies reveal generations of humble farmers interspersed with occasional scholars. This agrarian ancestral past is in fact the collective cultural identity of the average Hongkonger—after all, many of our traceable ancestors came from places no farther away than the Pearl River Delta region of southern Guangdong, whose society and culture were similar, and in many cases identical, to those found in the New Territories.

The history of the indigenous villagers of the New Territories can serve as one of the sources of Hong Kong's cultural identity. Until relatively recently, this history was mainly preserved in genealogical records, and published piecemeal in relatively obscure academic books and journals, many of which are in Chinese. What this book aims to do is to assemble a detailed history, in English, of the two oldest and most representative villages in the New Territories. History is an interpreted truth, and its interpretation is almost always tinted by the cultural and political biases of its interpreters, be they local villagers or history scholars. This is especially the case with history during the colonial period, and the Chinese and the British have each written slightly different versions of the same stories. They could all be telling the truth, or, rather, the perceived truth derived from the narrow perspective from which the events were viewed and interpreted. This book tries to restrict the authors' own conscious and

Fig. 2 Bilingual road sign giving directions to Shui Tau Tsuen and Shui Mei Tsuen. With the West Rail Project and ensuing urban development, the future of Shui Tau Tsuen and Shui Mei Tsuen as clan-based village communities is at stake. *(Lee Ho Yin)*

unconscious biases by constructing the events based on contemporary records, rather than retelling the stories through second-hand reinterpretation of historical documents.

History, however, is only part of the picture. Equally important are the traditional village customs, beliefs, and practices passed down from the past and, hopefully, continuing into the future. These traditions are the soul of a village, the intangible elements that bring life to the tangible ones—the physical setting and architecture, making it a truly living village instead of a dead museum piece. Many of these customs and practices are directly related to the villages' patrilineal social system, a cornerstone of social order and stability for villages in the past. However, being gender-discriminating in nature, these customs and practices have become a political liability for the indigenous villagers in the increasingly politically correct Hong Kong society.

What does the future hold for the indigenous villagers? Until the mid-20th century, the village way of life in the New Territories experienced little change from the way it had been during imperial times. Since then, a combination of post-war government policies, urban expansion, economic development, and modern socio-political ideologies has brought gradual but irreversible change to New Territories village society. For the two villages featured in this book, their physical environment in particular is now under threat by the HK$51.7 billion West Rail Project launched by the Kowloon–Canton Railway Corporation (KCRC) that will span a 30.5 km rail line across the western part of the New Territories by 2003. This rail line is only the beginning. With it will come additional roads and other infrastructure supporting a mega urbanization programme that will transform many areas in the western New Territories into New Towns—mini satellite cities that can accommodate a population of over a million, each built around a KCRC station along the West Rail line. The two subject villages happen to be in close proximity to one of these KCRC stations, which means for certain that they will be irreversibly consumed by the intense urban development that will take place in the destined New Town Centre.

A bigger concern than the eventual loss of the villages' physical environment is whether the cultural activities will be able to survive once the traditional physical setting is gone. This is a question open to all readers, who will surely deduce their own answers. We, the authors, hope this book will provoke and stimulate Hongkongers to think more about how best to sustain our cultural roots.

Fig. 3 View of Kam Tin along Kam Tin Road in early 2001, showing that the area is still relatively unaffected by the urban development that has occurred in many parts of the New Territories. *(Lee Ho Yin)*

CHAPTER ONE

Enter the Tang Clan:
History of Kam Tin until the Late 19th Century

Beyond the Villages: Kam Tin in Context

SHUI TAU TSUEN (LITERALLY 'WATER HEAD VILLAGE') and Shui Mei Tsuen ('Water Tail Village') are two archetypal villages found in the New Territories. Hidden some distance away from the main road and not especially charming in appearance, the villages attract few curious visitors. Yet, the villages' seeming ordinariness belies the fact that they are amongst the oldest, if not in fact *the* oldest, villages in Hong Kong.[1] Indeed, the villages of Shui Tau and Shui Mei have quite possibly been around for close to a millennium.

Written records relating directly to the history of Shui Tau Tsuen and Shui Mei Tsuen are extremely scarce. The villages are rarely mentioned in publications on the history of the New Territories, and, when they are, it is always with reference to the wider context of Kam Tin.[2] Even in the villages' genealogical records and the oral history from the memories of knowledgeable village elders, the history of Shui Tau Tsuen and Shui Mei

Figs. 4a & 4b Aerial photos of Shui Tau Tsuen and Shui Mei Tsuen taken roughly forty years apart, in 1949 and 1991. *(Survey and Mapping Office, Hong Kong)*

Tsuen always relates to the history of Kam Tin. It is perhaps not surprising that the villages' history and identity have always been overshadowed by the wider historical and socio-cultural contexts of Kam Tin. As in a typical Confucian society, individuals are subservient to the greater collective, and individual identities can only find meaning from the collective whole. Hence, the history of the two villages must really be understood from the history of Kam Tin itself.

Information relating to the early history of Kam Tin is, however, also limited and sketchy. The earliest traceable history of Kam Tin goes back to the last dynasty of the Five-dynasty Period (907–960), the dynasty of Hou Zhou (951–960). As the area was occupied by the families of the Chan clan, it was naturally known as Chan Tin, or 'fields of the Chans'.[3] Later, Chan Tin gave way to Shum Lei, or 'Alley amidst High Hills'. This is an apt description of the local topography, which is a long strip of flat valley surrounded by hill ranges with peaks over 500m high. Only in the northwest direction does a break in the hill range provide an unobstructed skyline towards Deep Bay. With its natural flatness and almost all-round protection by mountains, what better place than here to build an airfield? Such a thought must have crossed the minds of military surveyors, and the result is Shek Kong Airfield, whose runway fits snugly into the topography of the land. When the fertile and well-irrigated valley became cultivated, Shum Lei became the equally descriptive Shum Lei Tin, or 'Fields in the Alley amidst High Hills'. But the slightly cumbersome name did not stick, as the locals preferred to shorten it to Shum Tin, or 'Fields amidst High Hills'. That abbreviated name stuck, and remained in use when the first of the Tang (*Deng*) clan settled in the valley in 973. As the Tang clan flourished and dominated Shum Tin, they became synonymous with the history of this area. As will be told later, it was thanks to the Tangs that the humble Shum Tin, a mere 'Alley amidst High Hills', became the prosperous Kam Tin, or 'Fields of Splendour'.

Genesis: The Founding of Kam Tin

IN ONE OF OUR EARLY VISITS TO THE VILLAGES, we asked a local villager for directions to the house of our contact, Mr. Tang. 'Which Mr. Tang?' he asked. With an expression that clearly indicated an effort to remain patient, he continued, 'Are you aware that we are all Tangs here?' That was our first social blunder in the villages. Kam Tin is the heartland and original homeland of Hong Kong's Tang clan. Walk into any of the villages in the Kam Tin area, and the chances are that the first person you bump into is a Tang. Among the five major clans in the New Territories,[4] the Tang clan is the largest and the wealthiest, and therefore the most socio-politically powerful. Among the fifteen major villages in the Kam Tin area, ten of them belong to the Tang clan.[5] Of these ten villages, Shui Tau Tsuen and Shui Mei Tsuen are historically the most significant, for they are the original villages founded by the first Tangs in Hong Kong. This means that the two villages are probably the oldest living villages in the whole of Hong Kong. Surprisingly, this significant historical fact about the villages is not widely known among people in Hong Kong.

Who are the Tangs? Where did they come from? Since the whole notion of clanship is based on ancestry and lineage, the Tangs' perspective of the past is directly related to who their founding ancestors were. Hence, the history and origins of the Tangs must necessarily be traced from their prominent ancestors. According to the Tangs' genealogy,[6] their grand ancestor was a man known as Tang Man (*Deng Man*), whose adult name was Tak-yeung (*Deyang*).[7] He was believed to be the twenty-sixth generation descendant of the mythical first Chinese emperor Huang Ti ('Yellow Emperor'), and the youngest son of emperor Zuding of the prehistoric Shang dynasty (about 16th century BC to about 11th century BC). According to genealogical records,[8] in 1324 BC Tang Man was the Grand Duke of the Kingdom of Deng in today's Hebei province, and henceforth his descendants adopted the surname Deng (which is Romanized as 'Tang' in Hong Kong).

Given that the ancient history of China is often a mixture of myth and fact, one cannot help but wonder about the authenticity of this three-millennium-old curriculum vitae. A more plausible explanation of the Tangs' ancient lineage is given by the local historian Sung Hok-pang,[9] who traces the Tang clan's earliest ancestor to one Tang Yue (*Deng Yu*), a native of Xinye province (today's Henan province) who lived from AD 2 to AD 58.[10] Tang Yue was an important person of his time. It is believed that he was a general in the Han dynasty (206 BC–AD 220), who helped subdue the rampant banditry that ravaged the country. In recognition of his accomplishments, Emperor Guangwu appointed the twenty-three-year-old Tang Yue as Prime Minister in AD 25. Forty-seven generations later, the descendants of Tang Yue had migrated from Henan to the county of Jishui in Jiangxi, the province just north of Guangdong. It was at this point that one of Tang Yue's direct descendants, Tang Hon-fat (*Deng Hanfu*), a scholar and junior official from the village of Baishacun, decided to migrate farther south. Some time during the early Song dynasty (960–1279), possibly in 973,[11] Tang Hon-fat resettled in Guangdong province, where he became the founding ancestor of the Tang's lineage in Guangdong.

The story of the Tang clan in Kam Tin begins with Tang Fu (*Deng Fu*), the great grandson of Tang Hon-fat, who was also known by his adult name of Tang Fu-hip (*Deng Fuxie*). He was the first Tang to settle in Kam

Tin in the early 12th century, and, consequently, he is regarded as the founding ancestor of the Tangs in Kam Tin as well as the whole of the New Territories. It is remarkable that the Tangs in Hong Kong can pinpoint their ancestry to a single individual who lived over three-quarters of a millennium ago. Who was Tang Fu? Was he an actual person or a figment of the villagers' imagination? Sceptics may rightly point to the many instances of folklore and legends being confused and perpetuated as historical facts, but this is certainly not the case with Tang Fu. The story of his emigration to Kam Tin and subsequent founding of the Tang clan in this area was recorded in *Xin'an Xianzhi* (Gazetteer of the Xin'an County), more commonly known in Hong Kong as the *San On Gazetteer*.[12]

Gazetteers of imperial China are no ordinary compilations of anecdotes; they are encyclopaedic handbooks containing factual information pertaining to the history, geography, economy, government, and culture of a particular locality (usually a county). Published under imperial edict, these gazetteers were revised and updated from time to time. Officials assigned to administer unfamiliar faraway places depended upon such gazetteers to acquaint themselves with the local context. In the 1819 edition by scholar Wang Chongxi, the gazetteer records a passage on Tang Fu and how he came to settle in Kam Tin:[13]

> Tang Fu, whose adult name is Fu-hip, a native of Jishui county in Jiangxi province, was awarded the degree of *jinshi*[14] and appointed to the post of *Chengwulang*[15] during the Changning period [1102–1106] of the Song dynasty. He was assigned to administer the county of Yangchun in the south, whose beautiful land and scenic landscape brought him to settle in Kam Tin below the hill of Kwai Kok Shan. There he founded the Lik Ying School to promote education, an account of which was written by Huo Wei of Nanhai. . . .

The place below the hill of Kwai Kok Shan[16] mentioned in the gazetteer is where Shui Tau Tsuen and Shui Mei Tsuen are found today. According to the inscription on his tombstone,[17] Tang Fu passed the examination for the *jinshi* degree—the highest educational qualification in imperial China—in the second year of the Changning period, which corresponds to the year 1103. As a member of the educated elite, he was concerned about the prospect of education for his descendants. Since there were no educational facilities in the vicinity, he went on to establish a traditional school that prepared young men (only men were formally educated in imperial China) for the early stages of the imperial examinations. This early school in Kam Tin, which no longer exists, would become the first ever school featured in the history of Hong Kong.

Traditionally, the Chinese believed (and still do, to some extent) that ancestral burial sites with good feng-shui would have positive influences on future generations. Tang Fu, being an accomplished scholar as well as an expert in the art of feng-shui, spotted three hill sites with particularly excellent feng-shui qualities, and he quickly relocated the graves of his previous three generations of male ancestors to these places. Tang Fu's

Fig. 5 Classroom of Shui Tau Tsuen's 19th century Yi Tai Study Hall. It is a traditional village school in which, during the Qing dynasty, Confucian classics were taught to young males in preparation for the entry-level imperial examination. The building was restored by the Antiquities and Monuments Office in a project from 1992 to 1994. *(Lee Ho Yin)*

great-grandfather Tang Hon-fat was reburied in Ah Kai Shan (at Yuen Long), his grandfather in Shan Pui (also at Yuen Long), and his father in Tso Kung Tam (at Tsuen Wan).[18] By reburying the bones of his three immediate male ancestors in his settled land, Tang Fu immediately created a strong lineage base from which his future family line could extend and branch out.

Tang Fu's burial strategy had far-reaching implications for future generations, as one of the traditional ways of settling disputes and claims of land ownership was by means of the locations of one's ancestral graves, and such a system of verifying land ownership is still a legally recognized practice in the New Territories. After his death, Tang Fu was buried with his wife on the hill of Kai Shan (also known as Ah Kai Shan) in Wang Chau, located about 5 km to the west of Kam Tin. Naturally, the gravesite is said to have the most excellent feng-shui. By choosing to be buried in the land

Fig. 6 Family graves in the village burial ground to the northeast of Shui Tau Tsuen and Shui Mei Tsuen. Important ancestral graves are elaborately built and carefully maintained, as ancestral burial sites have always been a means of establishing land ownership for New Territories clans. *(Lee Ho Yin)*

he had settled rather than his native homeland in Jishui, Tang Fu established himself as the ancestor to whom all future members of the Tang clan in Kam Tin, as well as in the New Territories, trace their lineage.

Pak Wai and Nam Wai: The Tangs' First Villages

TANG FU HAD TWO SONS, one of whom, Tang Po (*Deng Bu*), remained in Kam Tin, while the other, Tang Yeung (*Deng Yang*), settled in Dongguan. Po and Yeung each had one son, Sui (*Rui*) and Kwai (*Gui*). It is believed that the two cousins had a dispute that caused the formation of the second village in Kam Tin. Whatever really happened, Sui remained in the original village founded by his grandfather Fu, while Kwai set up another village to the south of the Kam Tin River. To distinguish the two villages, they were respectively named Pak Pin Wai ('North Side Village') and Nam Pin Wai ('South Side Village').[19] Today, while the original villages are long gone, their names have stuck in the mind of the villagers, who still refer to the two divided territories as Pak Wai ('North Village') and Nam Wai ('South Village').

Where exactly are Pak Wai and Nam Wai today, we wondered. It was not difficult for us to figure out where Pak Wai was, since current maps and street directories plainly identify the villages of Shui Tau Tsuen and Shui Mei Tsuen collectively as Pak Wai. Nam Wai, the South Village, on the other hand, was a bit of a mystery to us, since published materials on Kam Tin did not seem to agree with each other regarding its location. We found in one secondary reference that Nam Wai was an extant village called Kam Shui Tsuen, or 'Splendid Water Village'.[20] Failing to locate the village name on new as well as old maps and street directories, we put on our hiking shoes and went to ask the locals. Every villager we stopped and queried invariably replied with a blank look on their face, followed by a shake of the head. We went to Kam Hing Wai, a small village immediately to the south of Pak Wai, whose name sounded close enough to make us wonder if it was known as Kam Shui Wai in former times. A large man from the first house, awakened by the fierce barking of his dog, answered our query irritably, 'No, this village has always been Kam Hing Wai; there is no Kam Shui Wai in this area.' Well, that piece of information about Nam Wai must be wrong then, we concluded.

Fig. 7 An enormous man-made water channel to the south of Shui Tau Tsuen and Shui Mei Tsuen, which diverted the water flow from the natural course of the meandering Kam Tin River that once separated Pak Wai and Nam Wai. This modern engineering work is part of a multi million-dollar drainage project to eradicate flooding in the northwest New Territories. *(Lee Ho Yin)*

Another secondary source suggested that Pak Nam and Nam Wai were, respectively, today's Shui Mei Tsuen and Shui Tau Tsuen.[21] This seemed logical enough, as Shui Mei Tsuen was to the north and Shui Tau Tsuen to the south, so we thought. We sought out the current Village Representative (the elected village chief) of Shui Mei Tsuen, Johnny Tang, to verify this. 'That's not correct', he said. 'Shui Tau Tsuen and Shui Mei Tsuen have always been Pak Wai; Nam Wai is somewhere else.' He waved at a bespectacled old man standing nearby to gesture him to come over. 'Ah, ask my Uncle Luk here, he knows the local history and he'll tell you where Pak Wai and Nam Wai are.'

The seventy-year-old Tang Po-luk, the younger brother of Johnny's father, walked us to the edge of Kam Tin River near the entrance to Shui Tau Tsuen. The knowledgeable old man pointed a finger to the north in the direction of Shui Tau Tsuen and Shui Mei Tsuen: 'Here is Pak Wai.' Then he turned around and made a grand sweep with his hand towards the south across the river. 'Everything over there is Nam Wai.' And so the mystery was solved. Pak Wai is where Shui Tau Tsuen and Shui Mei Tsuen stand today, and Nam Wai no longer exists, although the name remains a local reference for the collection of villages that have developed on the south side of the Kam Tin River. As we gazed southwards across the narrow winding waterway, things suddenly became clearer to us. In our minds, journeying through our imagination some 900 years back in time, we conjured up the scenario of one angry cousin Kwai stepping off the spot we were standing on and wading across the river with his family and possessions. Once across on the south bank, he claimed his own village territory, separated from his cousin's on the north bank only by the boundary of the river.

Accidental Royalty: The Tang who Married a Lost Princess

KWAI, FOUNDER OF THE SOUTH VILLAGE, HAD TWO SONS, Yuen-ying and Yuen-hei (*Yuanying* and *Yuanxi*), while his cousin Sui, head of the North Village, had three sons, Yuen-wo, Yuen-leung, and Yuen-ching (*Yuanhe*, *Yuanliang*, and *Yuanzhen*). It was from these five great-grandsons of Tang Fu, often referred to as the 'Five Yuens', that the five main branches of the Tang clan in the New Territories began.[22] Among the five, only Sui's son Yuen-leung remained in Kam Tin. This means that he lived in Pak Wai, which is today's Shui Tau Tsuen and Shui Mei Tsuen. Yuen-leung's brother Yuen-ching settled in Ping Shan, where he became the founding ancestor of the Ping Shan branch of the Tang clan, while his other brother and two cousins moved to Dongguan. Yuen-leung produced a son, Wai-kap (*Weiji*), and it was he, the great-great-grandson of Tang Fu and an ancestral villager of Shui Tau Tsuen and Shui Mei Tsuen, who changed the fortune of the Tangs. An outline of what happened is recorded in the 1819 edition of the *San On Gazetteer*:[23]

> . . . [Fu's] great-great-grandson Wai-kap, whose adult name is Tze-ming, married the princess of Emperor Gaozong [who reigned from 1127 to 1162]; and their descendants have become a prominent clan living in places such as Kam Tin, Lung Yeuk Tau, Ping Shan, Chuk Tsuen, and Ha Tsuen.

The story is told with slightly more details in the inscription on Wai-kap's tombstone:[24]

> Our lord ancestor Wai-kap, whose adult name was Tsz-ming, and also known as Kat Shan [Jishan], was the son of Yuen-leung. According to the gazetteer of Dongguan, the daughter of Prince Kang, who was later to become Emperor Gaozong, was evacuated to a faraway place because of the turmoil of war. She was married to the son of Tang Sin (the adult name of Tang Yuen-leung), who had earned merit for defending the emperor. As the war was still raging, our lord and the lady hid away in the village of Kam Tin. During the Shaoxi period (1190–1194), our lord died, and the royal lady dispatched her eldest son Lam to bring a letter to Gaozong [to inform of her whereabouts]. Our lord ancestor was bestowed the title of *Junma*, and was rewarded ten *qing* [equal to 1,000 Chinese acres, or 666.7 hectares] of farmland, as well as hill-land and ferry wharves . . . .

What these understated records fail to recount is the series of dramatic events that led to the royal marriage.[25] The story, which was of epic proportions, began in the final years of the Northern Song dynasty (960–1127), a turbulent time during which warriors of the Nüzhen tribe from the kingdom of Jin (Manchuria, or the province of Heilongjiang, as it is known today), more commonly known as the Tartars, invaded northern China. In 1127, Tartar soldiers broke through the gates of the imperial capital of Kaifeng, Henan province, and captured the last two emperors of the Northern Song dynasty (960–1127), Emperors Huizhong and Qinzhong, as well as the wife of crown prince Kang. Prince Kang, who would later become Emperor Gaozong, the founding emperor of the Southern Song dynasty (1127–1279), reigning from 1127 to 1162, was away fighting the Tartars elsewhere in China, so he was not captured. Another member of the royal family who escaped was a daughter of Prince Kang from his second concubine. Rescued by loyal servants of the imperial household and disguised as a commoner, the eight-year-old princess (some sources put her age as ten) began her long escape to a safe haven in southern China.

In 1129, after almost two years on the run, the princess' escape party reached the province of Jiangxi, where Tang Yuen-leung (*Deng Yuanliang*),[26] the great-grandson of Tang Fu, was serving as the official governing the local county of Gan. Yuen-leung was in the process of raising an army to march north to recapture the Song capital. By chance, the princess and her entourage found the camp of Yuen-leung's forces when they spotted their flags. As war between the armies of the royalists and invaders was still raging, the servants thought that it would be best to keep the princess' identity secret, and they told Yuen-leung that the young girl was a daughter of a senior court official. Yuen-leung took the girl into his protection, and, when the fighting ceased, he brought her back to Kam Tin (which was then still known as Shum Tin), where the princess, with her identity under veil, spent the rest of her childhood happily as an adopted member of Yuen-leung's family. What happened from this point on diverges into two versions of the story.

The first and more common version of the story is a straightforward classic Chinese tale not unlike those featured in Chinese operas. The story continues with the princess growing to marriageable age, and Yuen-leung arranging for her to marry his son Tang Wai-kap (who is sometimes known in literature by his adult name Tsz-ming, or *Ziming*). After ten years of marriage, the couple produced four sons, Lam (*Lin*), Gei (*Qi*), Wai (*Huai*), and Chi (*Zi*). By this time, a tentative peace prevailed as China was split between two parallel but rival dynasties that co-existed uneasily within the vast empire. The Tartar rulers established the Jin dynasty (1115–1234) and retained the old Song capital as their own, while survivors of the Song court, having retreated south, declared their continuing Southern Song dynasty (1127–1279) in the new capital of Lin'an (today's Hangzhou in Zhejiang province). Some time during the Shaoxi period (1190–1194), Wai-kap, at the age of sixty-five, died. The princess felt that it was time to unveil her identity and inform the royal household of her whereabouts. She dispatched her eldest son Tang Lam (*Deng Lin*) to the imperial court with a letter explaining her situation.

By now, the princess's father had long abdicated and passed on the throne to Guanzong, the princess' nephew. The emperor promptly acknowledged the princess's relation by declaring her Wong Ku, or Royal Aunt. For his effort to defend the emperor and protect the princess, Wai-kap was posthumously honoured with the title of *Junma* (roughly translated as 'Royal Husband', conferred on men who married women of direct royal descent), and his four sons were bestowed the title of *Guoshe* (roughly, 'Royal Juniors'). Other rewards followed, and, according to legend, the emperor decreed that the Tangs in Kam Tin would float wooden geese down the Kam Tin River and claim all the land along the river by which the dummy geese floated. The emperor also decreed that anyone who picked up the wooden geese would be bonded in lifelong servitude to the Tangs.[27] There is probably little truth to this legend, but, according to the Tangs' genealogy, Wong Ku and her sons were granted lands that would take care of their livelihood and burial. These included vast tracts of farmland, something in the order of a thousand *mu* (Chinese acres),[28] as well as coastland built with ferry wharves to generate income and hill-land for burial.

The second version of the story, as told by historian Sung Hok-pang, has all the complexity and unpredictability of events in real life. Realistic as it may seem, this version of the story is actually no more authentic than the previous version, since there is no way to verify either of them. The story recounts what happened after the princess was taken into the protection of Tang Yuen-leung, and lived happily with his family in Shum Tin:[29]

> . . . The princess found happiness and security in Kam Tin. She was like a daughter in Yuen Leung's house, helped with the household duties and was quite content. Eventually she revealed who her father really was, and Yuen Leung was very troubled as to what to do with her. However when she became of marriageable age the elders of the village advised him to marry her to his son Tsz Ming [the adult name of Wai-kap] which, as she was quite willing, he did.
>
> Meanwhile the fighting between the Tartars and the Sung had ceased. Peace was made and [Prince Kang] had now become the Emperor [Gaozong], who ordered that enquiries should be made concerning his daughter. All county magistrates throughout the Empire were instructed to help and when the official notice was posted up in the vicinity of Kam Tin, [Wai-kap] was much frightened at having married the princess without the emperor's permission. But the princess said, 'Do not fear. My life

was saved by the Tang family and I have willingly become your wife. Go and tell the county magistrate who I am.' When the official heard the news he came at once and did obeisance to the princess, and then sent a petition to the emperor. [Gaozong] ordered [Wai-kap] and his wife to come to the capital, where they stayed for about a year, but the princess pined for Kam Tin and begged to be allowed to return to the place of her adoption. So the emperor let her go, but first he bestowed on her many wharves in the district as 'powder expenses'; and a large area of hill and forestland as 'toilet expenses'. On the thirteenth day of the seventh month of the 8th year of Siu Hing [*Shaoxing*], A.D. 1138, they started back for Kam Tin. . . .

One story, two versions, of a bittersweet tale about a lost princess who married a commoner and turned the Tangs into accidental royalty. For us, the authors and researchers of the history of Kam Tin, the question remains whether Wong Ku (Royal Aunt) was indeed a real person, or simply a figment of the clan's collective imagination, concocted to lend prestige to the bloodline of the Tangs. Stupidly, we raised our doubts with a clan elder, whose eyes immediately flared into a how-dare-you-ask-such-a-question expression. We furiously back-peddled our way to safe shores by clarifying that we had little doubt of the authenticity of Wong Ku, but we, as scholars, needed concrete evidence to consolidate an obvious truth. Thankfully, our hastily concocted explanation managed to save us from our foot-in-mouth blunder, and our insulted villager immediately relaxed and resumed his usual friendly smile. 'Of course she was a real person, and if you don't believe me, you can go see her grave in Dongguan.' As the clan elder went on to elaborate the details of Wong Ku's grave, we could not help but smile at the inherent irony that the proof of Wong Ku's life had to be found in her place of death.

Wong Ku: Life and Death of a Princess

Indeed, the story of Wong Ku is not local folklore, but an important part of Kam Tin's history and the Tang clan's genealogy. After Wong Ku regained her royal status, she and her sons moved to Mojiadong in Dongguan, where she died in old age and was buried in the hills of Shiziling (Lion Ridge) near the village of Shijing, located to the southeast of today's Dongguan City. Anyone who visits Wong Ku's grave, which still exists, will find it prominently marked by a number of stone tablets. Most of these tablets were erected to commemorate major repair works carried out on the gravesite at various times, the oldest of which is one dating back to the Ming dynasty in 1570. In addition, there are two Qing dynasty tablets for repair work carried out in 1712, and another for work done as recently as in 1987.[30] The oldest Ming dynasty tablet purports to have reproduced the text inscribed on the original tombstone that no longer exists, and Wong Ku's life story is told in this text:[31]

> Our late mother, the daughter of Song emperor Gaozong, and wife of Royal Husband Tang Wai-kap, . . . was born on the 12th day of the 12th moon in the 29th year of the Shaoxing period [1159]. She died on the 7th day of the 2nd lunar month in the 5th year of the Chunyou period [1245], at the age of eighty-six. She was buried in the first moon of the following year in [the hills of] Shiziling in Shijing, facing the south-west direction, while Royal Husband was buried separately in Foaoling in Jiudu, facing the east direction.[32] The detailed account of her life story can be found in local historical records. The Song emperor Guangzhong had awarded her ten *qing* [equal to 1,000 *mu*] of land, which are now passed on to her surviving children. This tombstone was erected in great sorrow by her filial sons Lam, Gei, Wai, and Chi [*Lin, Qi, Huai,* and *Zi*], and filial grandson Yim-lung [*Yanlong*] on the first moon of the 6th year of the Chunyou period [1246]. . . .

Most of the information given on this tablet can be verified through physical proof (extant graves of Wong Ku and her husband) and documentary evidence (names of Wong Ku's children from the Tang genealogy). However, the dates given in the inscription are inaccurate; for example, Wong Ku's year of birth is given as 1159, which is not likely, since this would place her birth thirty-two years *after* the invasion of the Northern Song capital, the historic event that caused her to flee south and eventually settle in Kam Tin.

After Wong Ku returned to Kam Tin, she performed a charitable act by declaring her personal burial ground public property:[33]

> . . . the princess gave orders that the hills and woodlands should be thrown open to the public, so that anyone could make graves on her land without paying tax. In . . . A.D. 1712, when the princess' grave was repaired, her dowry was still being used by the country people for a free burial ground. . . .

However, this gesture of Wong Ku's generosity was overturned by one of her descendants, a Tang Gan-sze (*Deng Jinsi*) who, in 1686, erected a stone tablet in front of Wong Ku's grave warning against illegal burial. Traditional Chinese belief has it that a burial site with good feng-shui will have a positive effect on the deceased's descendants. Apparently, Wong Ku's gravesite was considered to carry such excellent feng-shui that it attracted a number of attempted illegal burials. With the backing of the local authorities, Gan-sze inscribed a lengthy warning in granite to forestall future infringement on his ancestral burial ground, an extract from which follows:[34]

> With permission of the Office of the Dongguan County, Guangzhou Prefecture, we seek to erect this tablet with a stern warning against illegal burial on this gravesite . . .
>
> As we live afar, we are weary of criminal gangs who conspire to steal burial plots within our auspicious ancestral burial ground. The crooked scheme they devise is unusually cunning in that they leave no noticeable trace of their illegal graves for many years, but they will later quietly set up tombstones and begin performing funeral rituals. My clansmen and I therefore have to think ahead and plead to the authorities to ban such illegal burials by our own people from Shijing or those belonging to other surnames from afar. Any illegal graves found, regardless of how old or recent they are, will be dug up, and the offending parties prosecuted. Any unfilial sons from Shijing who seek to steal and sell burial rights to outsiders will be dealt with according to the law. . . .

42 A TALE OF TWO VILLAGES

Today, some three-quarters of a millennium after the death of Wong Ku, memories of her are still very much alive among the Tangs in Kam Tin. On one visit to Kam Tin to find out more about Wong Ku, a friendly village elder led us to the Tangs' ancestral hall in Shui Mei Tsuen, a building with three halls and two courtyards. As we crossed the second courtyard, we came to the back hall where multi-layered rows of sacred ancestral tablets—timber plaques that represent shrines of ancestors—were arranged on three ancestral altars. With his right hand, the clansman directed our attention to the altar on the left and pointed towards the middle of the stacks. 'See that?' he asked in a soft, respectful voice as if he was speaking before someone highly important. 'That is the ancestral tablet of our Wong Ku, the only female who is allowed to have a tablet placed on the ancestral altar.' As we squinted our eyes to try to differentiate the Royal Aunt's tablet from the rest, he whispered again, 'It is the one with a dragon's

Fig. 8 Ancestral tablets, used for the worship of male ancestors, laid out in hierarchical order on the shrine of an ancestral hall in Shui Tau Tsuen. Wong Ku is the only known female ancestor in the New Territories honoured with an ancestral tablet. *(Information Services Department)*

head at the top.' Ah, we nodded as we spotted the unique tablet crowned with a tiny carving of a protruding dragon's head. The Tang clansman continued in his respectful whisper, but with a noticeable trace of pride in his voice, 'Because of her, we Tangs are descendants of royal blood.'

Fields of Splendour: The Naming of Kam Tin

DYNASTIES CAME AND WENT. The Southern Song dynasty collapsed in 1279 when the Mongolian armies of Genghis Khan successfully conquered the vast empire of China and established the Yuan dynasty (1206–1368). As the Cantonese saying goes, the mountain is high and the emperor is far away, and Shum Tin, being a remote place far from the imperial capital in the north, probably lived a quiet existence unmolested by the oppressive Mongolian regime. In 1368, the Mongolians were defeated by rebellious forces of the mainstream Han-Chinese people, and the Ming dynasty (1368–1644) came into being. In the 16th century, the county of Dongguan suffered a series of famines. Two particularly disastrous famines, which occurred in 1561 and 1568, brought large numbers of hungry and desperate victims to besiege towns in attempts to raid government granaries. The town of Nantou ('South Head', located in the south-western part of today's Shenzhen), one of the more populous in Dongguan county, felt particularly vulnerable at times of famine because it was far from the protective reach of the county capital. Community leaders of Nantou petitioned the provincial government to set up a separate county seat in their hometown. In 1572, their wish was granted by the emperor, and a new county with the auspicious name of Xin'an, which means 'New Peace' (commonly Romanized as 'San On' in Hong Kong), was established. The new county, with Nantou as the capital, roughly covered the territory of today's Shenzhen and Hong Kong.

In 1587, another famine, brought on by severe drought, broke out in the western part of Xin'an county. Government granaries in the county capital were soon emptied to relieve famine victims. Fearing the looming danger of civil riots by hungry peasants, the county magistrate made appeals in person to local districts for grain donations. The result was disappointing, to say the least, except for one particular donor, a Tang Yuen-fan (*Deng Yuanxun*) from the village of Shui Mei Tsuen in Shum Tin. As we shall see, the event was of such historic significance that it warranted an entry in the Tang genealogy:[35]

> In 1587, the west of Baoan [old name of Xin'an][36] suffered a disastrous drought, and, as a result, local government granaries were emptied. The county chief Qiu Tiqian personally went to the villages to seek donations of rice grains. The vast majority of donors contributed only three to seven *shi* [about 216 to 504 kg][37] of rice, and the generous ones no more than twenty to thirty *shi* [about 1,440 to 2,160 kg]. However, our revered Yuenfan (Yuanxun), who lived in the village of Shui Mei Tsuen, gave one thousand *shi* [about 72,000 kg], which impressed the county chief very much. On seeing the prosperous productivity of Shum Tin ['Fields amidst High Hills'], County Chief Qiu exclaimed how splendid the place was. He declared that it should be honoured with the name of Kam Tin ['Fields of Splendour'].

Fig. 9 The fertile flat plain of Kam Tin surrounded by high hills. Once a major agricultural area in the New Territories, Kam Tin is no longer the 'Fields of Splendour' it used to be. *(Lee Ho Yin)*

Thanks to a very charitable Tang from the village of Shui Mei Tsuen, the name given to the locality around the village was no longer a geographical description. It now became an honorific appellation to commemorate the extraordinary generosity of a man, and to celebrate the outstanding productivity of his land. This was the first time that Shui Mei Tsuen, or Water Tail Village, was mentioned in history. By Chinese place-naming conventions, where there is a tail, there ought to be a head, and vice versa. Hence, the mention of a Shui Mei Tsuen in the 16th century meant that there was also a Shui Tau Tsuen, or Water Head Village. It was at this point in time that the villages of Shui Tau Tsuen and Shui Mei Tsuen, Kam Tin, and the Tangs all became inseparable elements of an historic event.

War and Peace: The Impact of Dynastic Transition on Kam Tin

In the early 17th century, Manchu warriors rode into the Middle Kingdom and toppled the Ming Government, establishing the last of the imperial dynasties in China, the Qing dynasty (1616–1911). As in the case of all dynastic transitions in China, the period during the change from Ming to Qing brought great social upheaval as opposing armies fought each other at the expense of the ordinary people. Conquering and retreating soldiers alike took the opportunity to rape and plunder and kill those who got in their way. Troops of the defeated Ming power, being armed and having a bleak future under the victorious new Qing regime, resorted to banditry. They roamed like packs of wild dogs, raiding villages in places beyond the reach of the government military. The areas in southern coastal China were such places, and in Xin'an county, assaults on villages by large gangs of bandits were not uncommon. In 1647, a former army commander of the deposed Ming court by the name of Lee Man-wing (*Li Wanrong*) retreated with his surviving battalion to today's New Territories, where he made a stronghold until his surrender to the Qing Government in 1656. During his years of occupation, he and his soldiers looted and burned village after village, and turned many places in the New Territories into killing fields strewn with rotting bones. Only the villages of one particular place were spared the carnage, and that place was Kam Tin. Many believed that this was heaven's reward to

Fig. 10 The inner gateway of Tai Hong Wai, the first walled village in Kam Tin. *(Lee Ho Yin)*

Kam Tin for a noble act done by one of its native sons, Tang Man-wai (*Deng Wenwei*).

Tang Man-wai is featured prominently in the Tang genealogy. He was the only native person in the whole of the New Territories (that is, other than the clan's founding ancestor Tang Fu) to have passed the examination for the highest *jinshi* degree, which he did in 1685.[38] He was subsequently appointed to the post of magistrate for the county of Longyou in Zhejiang province, but died soon after of old age.

Yet Tang Man-wai was influential in another aspect of Kam Tin's history too. Some time back in the final years of the Ming dynasty, probably in the 1630s, it was said that Man-wai, then a young scholar, was on his way to collect rent from tenant farmers on his family's land when he came upon a young man who was beaten and hung upside-down from a tree. On enquiry, he learned that the young man was being punished for not paying his gambling debts. Man-wai, being an exceptionally kind-hearted person, took pity on the young man. Not only did the kind scholar repay the stranger's debts, he also found him a job in the army. As fate would have it, that debt-ridden gambler was Lee Man-wing.[39]

Although a brutal robber warlord in the New Territories, Lee Man-wing did not forget the scholar who had rescued him from ruin and probable death. Legend has it that he not only forbade his marauding soldiers to go near Kam Tin, but he also advised Tang Man-wai to build protective walls around his village to defend it against other marauders. Such close friendship between Tang and Lee would certainly have aroused conspiracy theories about their relationship. Indeed, there are sinister suggestions that the legend is merely a cover story to disguise the scholar's collaboration with the bandits.[40] Other stories, however, portray Man-wai as a hero who successfully defended Kam Tin from Lee Man-wing's bandit gang. What is indisputable is that Tang Man-wai was responsible for initiating the construction of one of the first fortified walled villages in Kam Tin—Tai Hong Wai, the village in which he was born. While some believe that the fortification work was carried out during Lee Man-wing's occupation of the New Territories (1647–1656),[41] most sources date the construction to the early reigning years of the Qing emperor Kangxi (1662–1722), which means that it would have been after the Coastal Evacuation Order was withdrawn in 1669.

The events that brought on the Coastal Evacuation Order began in 1661. By this time, the Manchus had firmly imposed their rule on almost the whole of China. However, there still remained pockets of stubborn resistance by remnants of the Ming army, in particular the 70,000 strong rebel forces under the command of the former Ming general, Zheng Chenggong (who is often referred to in Western literature as Koxinga), who were operating along the coastal areas of southern China. In 1661, General Zheng and his naval forces (which the Qing Government referred to, not inaccurately, as pirates) captured the island of Taiwan from the Dutch, who had seized it and used it as a military base and trading post. Zheng intended the island as a secure base to launch offensives on the mainland to recover the Ming empire from the Manchus. Naturally, the Qing emperor Shunzhi would not allow that to happen, and he immediately acted to nip Zheng's plan in the bud by denying him the material supplies and socio-economic support he would receive along the southern China coasts. The peaceful, prosperous county of Xin'an would soon feel the full force of the emperor's wrath.

In the eighth lunar month of the eighteenth and final year of the reign of Emperor Shunzhi (1661), the Coastal Evacuation Order was issued to turn southern China's coastal areas into militarized zones. Under this order, the coastal populations of the provinces of Jiangnan, Zhejiang, Fujian, and Guangdong would be forcibly moved inland to a distance of 30 to 50 *li* (equivalent to about 15 to 25 km). Forts and other defences would be constructed within the evacuated zones, and garrisons would be stationed at regular intervals along the inland boundaries. Guangdong was placed under the 50 *li* evacuation order, which covered almost the entire New Territories. In the evacuated zone, a scorched-earth policy was implemented to destroy fields and properties in order to deny the enemies food and shelter. Large numbers of government troops descended upon the coastal population to enforce the imperial order. People were driven away from their homes and went inland, while their farmland was burned, houses were demolished, and boats were sunk behind them. Those who refused to move were simply killed. The ones who moved fared no better; without land to farm, boats from which to fish, and communities with whom to trade, many of them soon starved and died. Corrupt officials and soldiers also exploited the situation to rob and extort villagers who were forced to relocate inland. One local genealogy recorded that 'those who had money were not harmed, but those who did not were left to die'.[42] As recorded in the *San On Gazetteer*, the fate of those who did not have the means to resettle elsewhere was grim:[43]

> . . . young children were sold off cheaply; a bushel of rice grains for a boy and one hundred copper coins for a girl. Some were forced to join the army, while others, feeling hopeless, took poison or drowned themselves in the river. It was also common for entire families to commit suicide. The world had turned into the ultimate tragedy. . . .

The coastal evacuation strategy, however, did not achieve the military objective of starving out General Zheng's rebel forces, which continued to roam freely along the coastal waters of the South China Sea. Three years later, in 1664, the new emperor Kangxi issued a second Coastal Evacuation Order to clear another 30 *li* of coastal land. With this order, the evacuation zone extended beyond the New Territories to cover nearly the whole of Xin'an county. Nantou, the county capital, came within the evacuation zone, and it was abandoned. What little was left of the areas not placed within the evacuation zone merged into the Dongguan county administration, and Xin'an ceased to exist. Kam Tin, like the rest of the land in the dead county, became a desolate wasteland of overgrown fields and crumbling houses.

In 1666, Wang Lairen was appointed Governor of Guangdong Province. On learning the disastrous effect of the coastal evacuation, he wrote a petition in 1668 to persuade Emperor Kangxi to withdraw the order:[44]

> With the coastal areas [of Guangdong] twice evacuated, tens of thousands of people have lost their homes, and the annual land revenues that are lost amount to over 30,000 taels of silver. On top of this, we spend large amounts of money, labour, and

materials every month and every year to defend the evacuated areas with troops and fortify it with forts and other defences. While those who were not evacuated live a hard life, those who were deprived of shelters have died in abundance. What gain do we achieve from this?

I plead for the immediate lifting of prohibitions imposed on the coastal areas so that people can return to farm and make salt, and for the removal of barricading piles in harbours and rivers so that people can return to fish. To defend our coast from external threat, I seek for the re-deployment of troops from interior regions to coastal prefectures and counties. This not only serves our national defence interest better, it also benefits the people by not requiring them to abandon their ancestral land.

One may argue that the consequence of the coastal evacuating is trivial compared to the issue of defending the coasts. While I can appreciate the original reasons for defending our borders and safeguarding our resources from the pirates, it is bad strategy to do so by driving people from homes and forcing them to retreat inland. In my two years or so as Governor of Guangdong, I have not come across any report of serious piratical incursions. What I have come across are reports of people evacuated from the coasts, driven by hunger, banding together as bandits. If these bandits are allowed to return home and resume production, they will surely be glad to trade swords for ploughshares.

The emperor probably realized what Wang was implying in his petition: the heavy-handed coastal evacuation strategy was not working as planned, and, worse still, it had sown the seeds for potential internal revolt as desperate and resentful refugees had armed and organized themselves into violent criminal gangs. Wang's petition was at once accepted and orders were issued to reverse the coastal evacuation policy. But just before the reversal process began, Wang fell ill and died. The task of implementing the de-evacuation fell to Zhou Youde, the Viceroy of the provinces of Guangdong and Guangxi. In 1669, a formal order to restore the evacuated coastal areas was issued, and displaced villagers were finally allowed to return home. For their noble deed, Wang and Zhou would be remembered by survivors of the coastal evacuation and their descendants. The two officials would be enshrined as gods and be worshipped in temples built in their honour.

Aftermath: The Changing Demography and Habitat in Post-evacuation Kam Tin

The coastal evacuation had almost completely depopulated the county of Xin'an. By 1669, the total population of the entire county was reduced to a mere 2,000, which is, to put it in perspective, about twice the present population of Shui Tau Tsuen and Shui Mei Tsuen combined. Despite official sanction to bring home the evacuated villagers, the county only managed to receive a trickle of 1,648 returnees by 1673.[45] The sad truth was that most of the 'evacuees' had already perished during the course of eviction from their homeland. One local genealogy painfully recorded that only twenty to thirty percent of their clanfolk had survived the ordeal.[46]

Figs. 11a, 11b, & 11c A series of three photos showing the gateways of Kat Hing Wai, Tai Hong Wai, and Wing Lung Wai. The fortified walls of Kat Hing Wai have remained more or less intact, while those of Tai Hong Wai and Wing Lung Wai are almost completely gone, but their gateways have survived. *(Lee Ho Yin)*

The low population level in Xin'an county had serious socio-economic implications for sustaining sufficiency in agricultural production and providing revenue from taxation for the local and provincial governments.

To help revive Xin'an county's population level, people from places outside the county were encouraged to move in with incentives of free land and properties. Such an enticing immigration package attracted many Hakkas (literally 'Guest Families', a euphemistic reference to their outcast status in their adopted homeland in southern China), who seized the opportunity and migrated en masse into Xin'an, changing the county's demographic nature forever. In 1773, about a century after the end of the coastal evacuation, the population of Xin'an had risen to over two hundred thousand people,[47] a large number of whom were immigrants. By this time, Xin'an boasted 366 immigrant villages, 345 of which were of Hakka ethnicity, thus showing the extent of the Hakka migration into the area that would become modern-day Shenzhen and the New Territories.

The Hakkas were a people originally from central China who migrated to the southern provinces of Guangdong and Fujian around the 10th century. As a people proud of their language and traditions, they did not assimilate themselves with the mainstream cultures in southern China. As such, they were never quite welcomed by the majority Cantonese and Hokkien speaking people in Guangdong and Fujian, who regarded them as 'outsiders'. Partly to preserve their own culture, but mainly to protect themselves from violent acts of xenophobia, the Hakkas tended to live away from the mainstream populations on poorer land and in huge fortified communal buildings. Most of the early Hakka immigrants who came to settle in the New Territories were from the Hakka heartland in eastern Guangdong, particularly from the counties of Huizhou and Chaozhou.[48] They were mostly subsistence farmers who, for generations, had been scratching a meagre living on rugged hill-land along the upper reaches of the rivers of Dongjiang and Hanjiang. They came with hopes and dreams offered by official promises of better land, more food, and special quotas in the imperial examinations, which could lead to the wealth and status of which they were hitherto deprived.

Such socio-economic prospects were not lost on a number of opportunistic villagers who were of indigenous Cantonese origin (known as

Puntis, or 'Locals'), and they quickly exploited the situation and reaped the immigration benefits by claiming to be Hakkas.[49] This intentional blurring of ethnic origins by some Punti villages, and the subsequent inflow of Hakka tenancy farmers into Punti villages, has led to the present-day confused impression that many of the indigenous villages in the New Territories are of Hakka descent. When the British leased the New Territories in 1898, the New Territories had 423 villages, of which 161 were Punti, containing 64,130 villagers, and 225 were Hakka, containing 36,070 villagers.[50]

As the Tangs returned to Kam Tin in 1669, they immediately went about rebuilding their homeland. Tang Man-wai, holder of the *juren* title (the second-highest academic qualification in Qing-dynasty China, which he attained in 1657) and the future holder of the most esteemed *jinshi* title (he would pass the examination in 1685), was to become a leading figure in the post-evacuation reconstruction of Kam Tin. The first task was to revive the local economy. Since it was necessary to revive the market, which had been set up in a place called Tai Kiu Tun (Today's Tai Kei Leng, southeast of Yuen Long), Man-wai took the opportunity to rebuild it in a new site whose land was (and still is) owned by Kam Tin's Tang clan. This meant that Man-wai and his clansmen had direct control of the market and therefore stood to gain most economically. Such a major business manoeuvre would not have been possible without his influence and connections as an advanced scholar (educated people were highly respected in imperial times). The market, which is today's Yuen Long Kau Hui (also known as Yuen Long Old Market), would become the largest commercial venue to the south of Nantou, the capital of Xin'an county, at the end of the 19th century.

The next urgent rebuilding task was defence. Like the rest of the New Territories, Kam Tin was not sufficiently important to warrant troop protection, and the villagers were left to fend for themselves. Attacks by pirates and bandits were a persistent threat, and would remain so until the early 20th century when the British established regular policing in the New Territories.[51] In addition, there was the ever-present concern of clan feud, and the Tangs, as a wealthy clan of people controlling much of the local economy, needed to guard against jealous neighbours and disgruntled rivals. Some time during the 1670s, Tang Man-wai and fellow villager

Tang Gai-yue (*Deng Jieyue*) began to fortify their home village Tai Hong Wai ('Peace Health Village'; extant).⁵²

They had the village enclosed in a thick square belt of heavily fortified walls built of hard grey bricks, with gun ports at regular intervals, watchtowers at the corners, and a moat all around. Heavy cast-iron canons protruding menacingly from gaps along the parapet walls helped further to deter would-be attackers. Other villages in Kam Tin quickly followed suit to fortify and arm themselves in similar fashion. These villages included Kam Hing Wai ('Splendid Joy Village'; extant), Kat Hing Wai ('Luck Joy Village'; extant), and Wing Lung Wai ('Forever Prosper Village'; extant). All of these villages were founded during the reign of the Ming emperor Chenghua (1465–1487), and they only became walled villages during the reign of the Qing emperor Kangxi (1662–1722). One of the walled villages, Kat Hing Wai, would become the scene of a famous battle between local militias and British troops in the late 19th century, when the British leased a part of Xin'an that included Kam Tin.

As life in Kam Tin returned to normal, it was time to pay tribute to Governor Wang and Viceroy Zhou, the men to whom the Tangs were indebted for their community's post-evacuation resurgence. In 1685, the year in which Tang Man-wai was awarded the *jinshi* title, a school was built in remembrance of Wang and Zhou. It was a most appropriate gesture, given that Kam Tin was founded by a scholar. The school, Chou Wong Yi Kung Shue Yuen (*Zhouwang Ergong Shuyuan*), which literally translates as 'Study Hall of the Two Lords Zhou and Wang', still extant, stands alone on a field at the southeast fringe of Shui Tau Tsuen. To heal their collective psychological wound, the Tangs of Kam Tin launched a community-wide religious ceremony known by the Cantonese name of Da Chiu. Held once every ten years since 1685 on the open ground in front of Zhou and Wang's memorial school, the ceremony offers prayers and offerings to pacify the many embittered spirits of fellow villagers who lost their lives during the coastal evacuation.⁵³

After the coastal evacuation, Kam Tin experienced some two hundred years of relative peace before it was to face another crisis. The landmark events that led to this crisis began unfolding in 1842, when Hong Kong, a sparsely populated island some 20 km to the south of Kam Tin, was ceded to Great Britain, following China's defeat in the Opium War. In

1860, following the Second Opium War, Kowloon peninsula met the same fate. The British were now eyeing the New Territories. For the Tangs of Kam Tin, their first encounter with the British would turn out to be a clash of civilizations.

Notes

1. According to genealogical records as well as Chinese historical documents such as the *San On Gazetteer* (the 1819 edition by Wang Chongxi was translated by Peter Y. L. Ng (1983) as *New Peace County: A Chinese Gazetteer of the Hong Kong Region*), the first historically recorded Han-Chinese settler in today's Hong Kong territory was Tang Fu, the founding ancestor of the two villages and the entire Tang clan in the New Territories. To the best of the authors' knowledge, there is no record to show that there is an older surviving village in the territory of Hong Kong, although such a possibility may exist. Before the Tangs' arrival, the territory of Hong Kong, including the New Territories, is believed to have been sparsely inhabited by what is termed today as Chinese minority people, such as the nomadic Tanka fisherfolk, and possibly descendants of the ancient Yao race (who, today, would be termed a Chinese minority race), whose remains were excavated in 1997 on the island of Ma Wan (located about 12 km to the northeast of Hong Kong's Chek Lap Kok Airport).
2. The New Territories is currently administered under five districts: Sai Kung, Shatin, Tai Po, Tsuen Wan, Tuen Mun, and Yuen Long. Kam Tin is an area administered under the district of Yuen Long.
3. See: Sung 1973, 111.
4. The five great clans in Hong Kong's New Territories are: the Tang (*Deng*), the Hau (*Hou*), the Pang (*Peng*), the Liu (*Liao*), and the Man (*Wen*).
5. These ten villages of the Tang clan in the Kam Tin area (with 1960 population figures) are: Kam Tin Shi (205); Kam Hing Wai (population included with Kam Tin Shi); Kat Hing Wai (410); Ko Po (population included with Kam Tin Shi); Shui Mei Tsuen (250); Shui Tau Tsuen (665); Tai Hong Tsuen (population included with Tsz Tong Tsuen); Tai Hong Wai (215); Tsz Tong Tsuen (155); and Wing Lung Wai (250). See: Hong Kong Government 1960, 172–173.
6. See Leung 1980, 40.
7. In classical China, learned people had birth names as well as 'adult names', which they adopted at the age of twenty.
8. Traditionally, every clan village maintains a 'genealogical record' that details not only the clan's genealogy, but also important people, such as scholars who passed the imperial examinations and became officials, and historic events, such as wars and disasters. The genealogical record is updated every generation by a village scholar, and usually kept by the village patriarch. The record serves as the authoritative source

for individual clan members to trace their ancestral lineage and determine their land rights and other entitlements. In Hong Kong, it is legally acceptable to prove one's land right in a village by evidence given in the village genealogical record.

9   See: Sung 1973, 113.
10 According to Sung (1973, 113), Tang Yue was born in the second year of the reign of Western Han Emperor Pingti (AD 2) and died in the first year of the reign of Eastern Han Emperor Mingti (AD 58). This gives him a life span of 56 years, although Sung states that Tang Yue lived for 52 years.
11 See: Sung 1973, 114, and the essay 'The Tangs of Kam Tin' in the pamphlet *Yi Tai Study Hall* published by the Antiquities and Monuments Office (n.d.).
12 The areas known today as Hong Kong Island, Kowloon Peninsula, and the New Territories were administered under the county of San On (*Xin'an*) from 1573 onwards until they were taken over by the British in, respectively, 1842, 1860, and 1898.
13 Authors' own translation from the Chinese text reproduced in Fung 1996, 113. In Peter Y. L. Ng's *New Peace County* (1983, 119), there is a translation of the same passage, which makes an interesting comparison.
14 *Jinshi* is an academic qualification conferred after passing the palace examination by writing a thesis on a topic set by the emperor. In the Qing imperial examination system, a student must first pass the basic district-level examination before he (only men were allowed to participate in the examinations) could proceed to the provincial-level examination. Successful candidates of the provincial-level examination could proceed to the triennial metropolitan examination. Typically, every metropolitan examination would attract six to seven thousand candidates, of which only about three hundred would pass. Successful candidates then sat for the so-called palace examination, the highest-level examination held in the capital city. No candidate would be eliminated in this final examination. Instead, they were graded into three classes according to their results. The top three candidates were placed in the first class, and they received official appointments right away. Candidates graded in the second and third class had to sit for another examination before they were appointed to official posts. All candidates who sat for the palace examination held the academic title of *jinshi*. Roughly equivalent to a modern day university postgraduate degree, *jinshi* was the minimum academic qualification for appointment to the post of a magistrate (an official with administrative responsibilities and judiciary authority for a locality) or equivalent standing. See: Ho 1996, 10.
15 *Chengwulang* is a junior-rank official appointment that can be roughly translated as 'assistant (*cheng*) officer (*lang*) of government places (*wu*)'. In terms of duty and rank, it is probably comparable to an assistant district officer in the Hong Kong Government's bureaucracy.
16 Kwai Kok Shan ('Cassia Horn Hill') is the highest peak (585 m) in the range of hills known as Kai Kung Leng ('Cock's Ridge'), located to the northeast of Kam Tin. In some sources, such as in Siu 1989, 79, Kwai Kok Shan is confused with the adjacent hill of Kai Kung Shan (374 m).
17 For the full text of the inscription on Tang Fu's tombstone, see: Siu 1990, 42–43.

[18] See: Leung 1980, 74.
[19] See: Sung 1978, 205. The names Pak Pin Wai and Nam Pin Wai have been confirmed by local villagers.
[20] See: Siu 1989, 79.
[21] See: Fung 1996, 26.
[22] See: Siu 1990, 43.
[23] Authors' own translation from the Chinese text reproduced in Fung 1996, 113.
[24] Authors' own translation from the Chinese text reproduced in Siu 1990, 46–47.
[25] See: Fung 1996, 113, and Sung 1973, 121.
[26] Tang's birth name was Tang Sin (*Deng Xian*).
[27] See: Fung 1996, 114.
[28] A Chinese acre, or *mu*, is roughly 6.67 hectares; 1,000 Chinese acres are therefore equivalent to about 667 hectares.
[29] See: Sung 1973, 121–123; the story was originally published in the April 1936 issue of *The Hong Kong Naturalists*.
[30] The Chinese texts inscribed on these tablets are reproduced in Siu 1990, 47–51.
[31] Authors' own translation from the Chinese text reproduced in Siu 1990, 47–48.
[32] Fat Au Leng (*Foaoling*) is a small hill at Au Tau, which is about 1.5 km to the west of Shui Tau Tsuen and Shui Mei Tsuen, and Jiudu ('Nine Cities') was the contemporary (during the Southern Song dynasty) designation for the territory now known as Hong Kong. Until relatively recent times, the area known today as Hong Kong was a fairly insignificant and faraway corner of the vast empire of China. As such, there was no specific name attached to it, and it was known by different names in different times. In fact, place-names in the territory of Hong Kong, in both Chinese and Romanized versions, were not formalized until the publication of *A Gazetteer of Place Names in Hong Kong, Kowloon and the New Territories* by the Hong Kong Government in 1960.
[33] See: Sung 1973, 122.
[34] Authors' own translation from the Chinese text reproduced in Siu 1990, 47–51.
[35] The block quotation is the authors' own translation from the Chinese text reproduced in the Antiquities and Monuments Office's pamphlet *Yi Tai Study Hall* (n.d.). A slightly condensed version of the same text appears in Siu 1990, 41.
[36] The territory that is known today as Hong Kong was zoned under different county administrations at different times. Before the Tang dynasty, it was variously administered under the county seat of Panyu, Dongguan, and Baoan. During the Tang dynasty (618–907), it remained under Baoan county up to the year 757, when Baoan was absorbed into Dongguan. This was maintained well into the Ming dynasty (1368–1644) until 1572, when the southern part of Dongguan county was separated to become a new county administration called Xin'an (meaning 'New Peace', commonly Romanized as 'San On' in Hong Kong), which roughly covered the territory of today's Shenzhen and Hong Kong. This remained until the formation of the Chinese Republic in 1912, when the Republican Government reverted the county name of Xin'an back to the old name of Baoan. As historian Jason Wordie notes in his newspaper article 'When Hong Kong was New Peace County' (2001), 'It is still not uncommon for elderly New Territories villagers to refer to themselves as natives

of Po On [*Baoan*] District when naming their *heung ha* (ancestral village), rather than a specific part of the New Territories.' For details of Hong Kong's zoning throughout the imperial dynasties, see Leung 1980, 17–19.

[37] One *shi*, or 'stone', is about 72 kg.

[38] For Tang Man-wai's biography, see: Ho et al. 1996, 75 and p. 19, vol. 29 of the 1819 edition of the *San On Gazetteer*. The year in which Tang Man-wai obtained his *jinshi* degree is given as 1669 in some sources (e.g., Fung 1996, 38), which is incorrect. It would be highly unlikely for Tang Man-wai to have sat for the imperial exam in 1669, the year in which the Tangs of Kam Tin returned from the eight-year long exile during the coastal evacuation. The correct year is 1685, as indicated on p. 19, vol. 29 of the 1819 edition of the *San On Gazetteer*.

[39] The story of Tang Man-wai and Lee Man-wing is recounted in Sung 1974, 172–173.

[40] See: Kamm 1978, 210.

[41] For example, in Leung 1980,' 89.

[42] According to the genealogy of the Wan clan in Lung Yeuk Tau, Fanling; quoted in Faure 1984, 38.

[43] Recorded in vol. 11 of the 1819 edition of the *San On Gazetteer* by Wang Chongxi, and translated by the authors; see also: Lau 1999, 11.

[44] Authors' own translation from the Chinese text reproduced in Yau 1992, 63–64; the text is also found in vol. 11 of the 1819 edition of the *San On Gazetteer* by Wang Chongxi.

[45] See: Lau 1999, 11.

[46] According to the genealogy of the Wan clan in Lung Yeuk Tau, Fanling; quoted in Faure 1984, 38.

[47] See: Lau 1999, 11; the exact population figure given is 239, 112.

[48] For details of the origins of the Hakka immigrants who settled in the New Territories after the Coastal Evacuation, see: Siu 1990, 7–12.

[49] See: Siu 1990, 16, 33 n. 107.

[50] See: Lockhart 1898, section 'Inhabitants', paras. 3 and 4.

[51] See: Welsh 1993, 333.

[52] See: Sung 1974, 173 and Siu 1989, 79.

[53] See: Leung 1980, 44, 75. Kam Tin's last Da Chiu ceremony of the 20th century was held in 1995.

Fig. 12 Soldiers of the Hong Kong Volunteers manoeuvering their Maxim guns on wheeled carriages on hills in the New Territories in 1899. A small group of officers converse in the foreground (lower right) while a number of local Chinese villagers in the background calmly look on. *(Public Records Office, Hong Kong)*

CHAPTER TWO

The British are Coming:
The Union Jack over Kam Tin

Barbarians at the Gate: The British Arrive in Kam Tin

IN 1898, A PIECE OF CHINESE TERRITORY of about 974 km² north of Kowloon was forcibly leased to the British for a period of 99 years. The circumstances leading to what Prime Minister Lord Salisbury referred to as 'a slight extension to the colony of Hong-kong'[1] is neatly summed up in the words of historian Jason Wordie:[2]

> This was during the general scramble for concessions by other European powers in China when the French leased the port of Kwangchow-wan between Hong Kong and Haiphong, the Russians took over Port Arthur (modern Dalian), and the Germans were developing the city of Tsingtao. These expansions were motivated as much by a desire not to be outclassed by other European powers as by any hope of great economic gain.

Back in London, the British Government knew very little about the 'New Territory' (as it was initially called) and, as such, there was an urgent need to find out about this latest territorial acquisition of the British Empire. In late June 1898, at the suggestion of Joseph Chamberlain, the British Colonial Secretary, a Special Commission was set up to undertake this fact-finding task. The person designated to head the commission was James Haldane Stewart Lockhart, the Hong Kong Colonial Secretary and Registrar General, whose literacy in the Chinese language and 18 years of experience in the Hong Kong administration made him a natural candidate for the job. He was thus temporarily relieved of his duties and appointed the Special Commissioner.

Lockhart was on home leave in Southport when he received his orders, and he took off almost immediately for Hong Kong, arriving in Victoria Harbour in early August. Lockhart knew that he had a very tight schedule to meet: he had to complete his report and submit it to the Colonial Office in London by early October, before the new Governor of Hong Kong, Sir Henry Blake, was to assume office in November. Given the length of time taken to travel by sea between London and Hong Kong, Lockhart would have less than a month to complete his investigation before he set sail back to London. In the event, Lockhart would use the time during his return journey to complete his famous report.

The thirty-one-page document that came to be popularly referred to as the *Lockhart Report*, dated 8 October 1898, provides general but comprehensive insight into the land, the people, the economy, and the society of the New Territories as it existed in the late 19th century. For the most part, the *Lockhart Report* is an objective and impersonal reporting of facts and figures, as a government report should be. However, in one paragraph, Lockhart seems to have slipped in, perhaps unintentionally, his personal feelings concerning an unpleasant encounter during his inspection tour of the New Territories:[3]

> . . . During the inspection of the territory they [the villagers of the New Territories] gave us an excellent reception except in two instances one of which was so marked that it was necessary to bring the conduct of the villagers concerned to the notice of the

Viceroy of the Two Kwang who will, it is hoped, deal with the matter in a proper manner. . . .

The 'marked instance' mentioned in the report actually took place in Kam Tin. In typical British understated manner, the 'instances' are mentioned almost in passing, as if they warranted no further attention. But it could not have been a less than serious matter to require the British Government to file an official complaint to the Viceroy of the 'Two Kwang', the highest authority in charge of the Chinese provinces of Kwang-tung (Guangdong) and Kwang-si (Guangxi). While it is clear that Lockhart encountered something unpleasant in Kam Tin, what actually happened?

The story begins with Lockhart and members of his Special Commission entering the New Territories in August 1898, visiting villages, asking questions, and making records. As Lockhart reported, they were by and large given an 'excellent reception', but, in reality, they were more likely met with a mixture of traditional courtesy and bemused indifference. Occasionally, a show of shrewd diplomacy by showering naïve villagers with coins was often all that was needed to defuse animosity.[4] All was going well until the party navigated up the Kam Tin River in their steamer and arrived at Kam Tin. As the story goes, the clan elders of Kam Tin refused to meet Lockhart and had the commission's sedan chair bearers driven away, but the worst was yet to come. As reported in the 17 September 1898 edition of the *Hongkong Weekly Press*,[5] a thousand villagers showed up to welcome the commission with 'vigorously beaten gongs, but in place of chin-chins and flowers, they came with cries of *ta* [Cantonese battle cry that means "hit (them)"] and "foreign devils" '. In some accounts, there is mention of the commission being pelted with rotten eggs.[6]

It was not a good day for Lockhart, to say the least. The final insult for Lockhart came as he was bluntly refused entry to the walled village of Kat Hing Wai. According to a journal of the trip kept by Lockhart,[7] he managed to convince the inhabitants of Kat Hing Wai to open the pair of closed wrought-iron gates after giving them 'a clear explanation'. In reality, as the newspaper report mentioned above reveals, the 'explanation' was conveyed with a force of 75 Royal Marines and two Maxim

Fig. 13 The legendary chain-linked wrought-iron gates of Kat Hing Wai. Such gates were also installed in a number of other walled villages in the New Territories. One of Kat Hing Wai's gates originally belonged to Tai Hong Wai, while similar gates can still be found in Ma Wat Wai and San Wai in Lung Yeuk Tau, Northeast New Territories. *(Public Records Office, Hong Kong)*

guns.[8] The incident was duly brought to the attention of the Viceroy of Guangdong and Guangxi, and the matter was put to rest as a delegation from Kam Tin travelled to Hong Kong Island to present a formal apology to the authorities. However, the matter was far from being resolved. Lockhart's gunboat diplomacy tactics probably served only to confirm the Tangs' worst fear—that the British were coming to take away their land and properties. As Lockhart reported to the Houses of Parliament in November 1900:[9]

> One great difficulty has been suspicion on the part of the inhabitants of the intention of the Government. The people [in the New Territories] seemed to fear that the Government intended to take their land away from them . . . .

Thus, the first official contact between the British and the Tangs got off on the wrong foot, and it created a cross-cultural misunderstanding with tragic consequences.

In the two hundred years of ensuing peace after the end of the Coastal Evacuation in 1669, the Tangs of Kam Tin grew so prosperous and powerful that they became the de facto local authorities. As historian John Thomas Kamm notes, the Tangs of Kam Tin 'acted as "unofficial" government of a large section of the San On [*Xin'an*] county',[10] and they 'existed as a power often beyond the reach of the local magistracy'.[11] Meanwhile, the Qing Government, which had suffered one humiliation after another from the British, must have realized that the Tangs could be exploited to get back at the British. Hence, the Tangs were probably misinformed about the nature of the Sino–British lease agreement for the New Territories, and they were probably told that their land would be taken away by the British as the lease came into effect.

However, the British had always found it implausible that the Tangs could be so easily misled. As Lockhart questioned in his 1900 parliamentary report,[12]

> It may be seen peculiar that suspicion should have arisen, seeing that His Excellency the Governor informed the inhabitants both by proclamation [in Chinese, made before the takeover] and by

speech that the tenure of land would remain practically undisturbed, and that the Chinese authorities repeatedly notified the inhabitants that the tenure of land would remain the same as before, and that the rights of property would be respected.

What the British did not realize was that education among the rural population was restricted to a privileged or gifted few, and the vast majority of the villagers were illiterate farmers who had learned from experience not to trust the authorities. They were therefore vulnerable to misinformation and disinformation relayed to them by people who harboured their own political agenda and consorted with the Qing authorities.

There is evidence to support this conspiracy theory, as the Tangs themselves later admitted that they had been instigated by others to rise up against the British. To commemorate the restoration of the famous wrought-iron chain-linked gates to the walled village of Kat Hing Wai in 1925, a granite plaque was installed on the village wall by the gate. Although the plaque was removed during the Japanese Occupation of Hong Kong and could not be found after the war, the Chinese inscription on the plaque has been preserved on record, part of which reads as follows:[13]

> In the 24th year of the reign of Emperor Guangxu [1898], the Qing Government zoned the southern end of the Shenzhen River to Britain. At that time, the Qing Government did not make any clear announcement in advance. Because of this, many ignorant villagers were manipulated into rebellion when the British troops arrived. . . .

It is therefore probable that the Qing authorities, through their supporters in the Tang clan, hoped to stir up a popular uprising against the British in the New Territories. The scheme almost succeeded.

Rebel without a Cause: The Battle of Kam Tin

THE BRITISH WERE NOT READY TO ASSUME ADMINISTRATION of the New Territories when the lease came into effect on 1 July 1898, as they needed time to understand what they had got themselves into. They also needed time to sort out the complicated mess of political, legal, taxation, and administrative details. The northern boundary of the New Territories was one example of the complications—it was not settled until 14 March 1899 because of continual bargaining and bickering between Chinese and British officials. The change of the governorship of Hong Kong from Sir William Robinson to Sir Henry Blake in November 1898 further delayed the takeover process. Meanwhile, a Chinese land syndicate in Hong Kong was buying up land in the New Territories at bargain prices by inflaming the villagers' unfounded fear of the impending seizure of their land by the British.[14] This unscrupulous move by local Chinese businessmen alarmed the new governor, who realized the financial implications for the government when it had to resume private land in the New Territories for public use. The Hong Kong Government was therefore compelled to take over the administration of the New Territories hurriedly before the land syndicate did so in a literal sense. The takeover was set at 1:00 p.m. on April 17, 1899.

The events leading to the Battle of Kam Tin began three days before, in Tai Po on 14 April 1899.[15] On this day, Chinese rebels led by the Tangs started preparing defensive positions on the hills of Pan Chung in south-west Tai Po, where some matsheds (temporary structures of bamboo poles with mat covering) had been constructed by the British for use as a temporary police station. The flag-raising ceremony to symbolize the formal takeover of the New Territories was scheduled to take place on the grounds of the temporary police station. The rebel leaders must have got wind of the impending takeover, since the date was public knowledge in Hong Kong, having been decided by the Hong Kong Executive Council, and the Viceroy of Guangdong and Guangxi had been informed of it.

The rebels were high in morale but short on modern long-range weapons, being armed with a number of muskets and 12 muzzle-loaded light cannons. They dug trenches and prepared gun emplacements on the

Fig. 14 Sir Henry Blake, Governor of Hong Kong from 1898 to 1904, who appropriated the gates of Kat Hing Wai and Tai Hong Wai in 1899. *(Information Services Department, Hong Kong)*

hills, and, once they were in position, they merrily marked their positions with colourful banners and announced their presence with cheers, gongs, firecrackers, and gunshots. Coincidentally, Lockhart went to Tai Po on the same day and he was warned of the trouble by friendly village elders. Unaware of the magnitude of the problem, Lockhart only requested sufficient troops to protect the matsheds for the flag-raising ceremony.

On the following day, the Captain Superintendent of Police, Henry May, arrived with 22 armed policemen on a steamer. They were joined by a company of 125 men from the Hong Kong Volunteers (the Volunteer Corps) under the command of Captain Berger. Unknown to the British, the Tangs, who had secured tacit approval if not covert support from both the county authorities in Nantou and the provincial authorities in Guangzhou,[16] had organized a rebel force of over two thousand men drawn from village vigilante groups from the New Territories as well as Shenzhen, Shatou, and Dongguan. On reaching Pan Chung, the British security force discovered that the matsheds had been burnt to the ground and they found themselves coming under fire from the rebels on the surrounding hills. Fortunately for the British, the rebels, being positioned more than 800 metres away, were too distant to take accurate shots with their primitive weapons. The outnumbered British force quickly withdrew from the hills and sent for reinforcements.

On the morning of April 16, three companies of troops, each armed with a Maxim gun, arrived at Tai Po by sea. As the troops landed and prepared to assault the rebel positions, the escorting gunboat *H.M.S. Fame*, a 350-ton destroyer, unleashed heavy bombardment on the rebels. Needless to say, the rebel force was no match for the superior firepower and professional training of the British army. Seeing the rebels had been beaten back, Lockhart seized the opportunity and declared the flag-raising ceremony would be held that very afternoon—one day earlier than the announced takeover date. A small matshed and a short flagpole were hastily erected,[17] and, for security, a contingent of 400 soldiers of the Hong Kong Regiment marched into the ceremonial ground.[18]

Following the obligatory gun salute from two warships anchored off Tai Po, the Union Jack was hurriedly raised by Lockhart himself as a large group of friendly villagers unrelated to the Tang clan looked on with puzzled bemusement, wondering what the pomp and circumstance was

Fig. 15 The hastily staged flag-raising ceremony in which Hong Kong Colonial Secretary and Registrar General James Stewart Lockhart officially declared the British takeover of the New Territories as of 2:50 p.m., 16 April 1899. *(Public Records Office, Hong Kong)*

all about. Lockhart proceeded to read an official proclamation,[19] and declared that the British formally assumed control of the New Territories as of 2:50 p.m., 16 April 1899. However, the battle was not yet over. Immediately after the ceremony, British troops went on to pursue the retreating Chinese rebels. As they entered Lam Tsuen Valley, they were ambushed by the rebels from the hills above. After an hour's fierce fighting, the British managed to drive off the rebels. The battle continued for two more days, and ended with the Battle of Kam Tin.

The so-called 'Battle of Kam Tin' did not actually take place in Kam Tin, but near the village of Shek Tau Wai in Sheung Tsuen, which is about

Fig. 16 Artillerymen of the Hong Kong Volunteers in 1899, standing by their muzzle-loaded field cannons. Although Chinese rebels outnumbered British soldiers in the Battle of Kam Tin, they were outmatched by the professional training, discipline, and firepower of the British forces.
(Public Records Office, Hong Kong)

two kilometres east of Kam Tin. In two days of battle, the British forces beat the rebels at every encounter, and were pushing westwards from Tai Po towards Kam Tin. On 18 April 1899, about 2,600 rebels regrouped at Yuen Long and advanced towards the British forces at Sheung Tsuen to launch a counter-attack. The large contingent of rebels was easily spotted by the British as they marched boldly eastwards, with colourful unit banners flying, across the flat plain of Shek Kong (where the future runway of Shek Kong Airfield would be built). As they reached the village of Shek Tau Wai at Sheung Tsuen, the rebels were ambushed by British troops lying in wait in a dried riverbed (probably the Kam Tin River). The British let the rebels come within 300 metres before they opened a volley of fire. The result was confusion and panic for the rebels as a number of them were killed or injured. The survivors quickly scattered and ran for their lives. With that, the Tang rebellion fizzled out.

The reason why the final battle at Sheung Tsuen has become identified with Kam Tin rather than the actual site of the action is because of a significant event that took place in Kam Tin after the Sheung Tsuen battle. Lockhart, who was present at the battle, suspected that the Tangs of Kam Tin had taken a leading role in the rebellion. Later in the evening after the final battle, Lockhart ordered troops into Kam Tin to search for the culprits. As had happened eight months earlier, the troops were kept out of Kat Hing Wai by its pair of chain-linked wrought-iron gates. Contemporary Chinese texts often claim that the British blasted down the gates with heavy artillery, and took them away as war trophies.[20] That is not correct, since the gates would have turned into scrap metal if they had been shot down by heavy artillery. What actually happened is elaborated by Peter Wesley-Smith in his well-researched article *The Kam Tin Gates*:[21]

> On April 18 a party of sappers from the Hong Kong Regiment blew down the walls flanking the gates of both Kat Hing Wai and Tai Hong Wai [with gunpowder], and a few days later the villagers themselves, as an act of submission, carried the two pairs of gates to Flag Staff Hill (Tai Po). There they were admired by Governor Sir Henry Blake who, wrote Stewart Lockhart, 'instructed me to forward to him a pair of gates from Kam Tin'. This was duly done in May. . . .

Wesley-Smith also writes of a little-known detail about the gates:

> The two sets of handsome gates were both defective, one wing of each having suffered from the back-scratching of generations of itchy Kam Tin pigs. The remaining gates in good condition were combined to make a pair and were appropriated by Blake for 'Myrtle Grove', his home in the Irish county of Youghal.

Over the years, the battle at Sheung Tsuen has been all but forgotten, but the story of the 'Kam Tin Gates' has developed into something of a local myth and has come to be identified with the flawed heroism of the Tangs in Kam Tin in their uprising against the British. It would take another quarter of a century before the gates were returned to their place of origin.

Conciliation: Relations between the Tangs and the British during the Colonial Period

THE BRITISH TURNED OUT TO BE MORE BENEVOLENT than the Tangs had expected. Under the imperial Chinese laws, defeated rebels were dealt with by execution and the extermination of their clans. Instead of subjecting the Tangs to such harsh punishment, Governor Blake wisely adopted a policy of winning them over by encouragement and fair measures.[22] In any case, despite their initial violent animosity, the Tangs and the British were quick to adopt a conciliatory attitude towards each other as soon as the fighting was over. This was evident in Governor Blake's introductory address to Lockhart's 1900 report presented to the British Parliament:[23]

> A request was made to me by elders from Ping Shan, an important village in the centre of the April disturbances, that a school should be opened for the teaching of English; I promised to accede to their request, and intend to do so as soon as possible.

After the incident in 1899, Kat Hing Wai remained gateless. Twenty-six years passed, and although the bitter battle at Sheung Tsuen was already a faded memory, the missing gates remained fresh in the villagers' minds. In 1924, Tang Pak-kau (*Deng Boqiu*), a village elder of Kat Hing Wai, wrote, on behalf of his village, a very courteous letter to the serving Governor Sir Reginald Stubbs, asking for the return of the gates. The governor obliged and, through Lady Blake, the daughter of former Governor Blake, the gates were traced to her father's estate. In a strange twist of fate, the retired Lockhart, who was responsible for confiscating the gates from the Tangs, ended up being the one tasked with recovering them from Ireland and returning them to Kam Tin.

The gates were shipped back to Hong Kong to be restored at Kat Hing Wai at public expense. However, when the gates arrived in Kam Tin, villagers of Tai Hong Wai recognized one of the gates as their own and demanded their half. For a while, it seemed that Kat Hing Wai and Tai Hong Wai might end up with the ridiculous situation of having half a gate installed at their respective entrances. After lengthy negotiations, the elders of the two walled villages realized that the Tang clan would be a laughing stock if each village was to fight over half a gate, and there would be greater propaganda value for the whole clan if a complete pair of gates were seen to be returned and restored by the British. So it was decided that Kat Hing Wai would have the honour, probably because of the fact that it was the village elders of Kat Hing Wai who initiated the return of the gates.

At 4:30 p.m. on 26 May 1925, a formal ceremony to mark the reinstallation of the gates commenced amidst thundering Chinese firecrackers and a rousing British military band. For the occasion, Governor Stubbs presented a remarkably conciliatory speech, which began by recounting a delightfully understated version of the events that led to the removal of the gates from the walled village:[24]

Fig. 17 Sir Reginald Stubbs, Governor of Hong Kong from 1919 to 1925, who restored the gates to Kat Hing Wai in the last year of his governorship. *(Information Services Department, Hong Kong)*

> I am pleased to see this large assembly today. The beginning dates back to the year 1898 when the lease of the New Territories was handed over by China to Great Britain. At that time there was some slight misunderstanding, and the natives of Kam Tin village were not prepared to welcome the new Government with quite the enthusiasm which we had hoped. The result of the misunderstanding was the removal of the old gates, of which they were justly proud.
>
> I hope that during the twenty-seven years which have elapsed since that time we have come to know each other better, and that the village of Kam Tin has realized that our object in this territory is merely to do the best we can for the village and its inhabitants. Our relations have been of the most friendly character throughout this time, and therefore last year when I was reminded of the fact that the gates had been removed and was asked whether I could have them sent back, I had the greatest pleasure in obtaining them from England, where they have been kept, and restoring them to the village, as a mark both of

> our goodwill to the people and of our appreciation of the loyalty which has always existed in the territory.
>
> The people of the New Territories have deserved well of us by giving us every assistance, and I have much pleasure in bringing these gates back. The gates have, I believe, been in the village for several hundred years, and I hope they will remain for many hundreds of years, and the village will prosper in the future even more than it has done in the past.

In reply, as mentioned earlier, the Tangs returned the courtesy with equally conciliatory words inscribed on a granite plaque installed on the right-hand side of the newly re-installed gates, excerpts of which read as follows:[25]

> Now the 26th generation grandson Pak-kau wrote on behalf of our Wai to the Hong Kong Government, which conveyed the message to the British capital, and had the gates returned and re-installed for our security. All expenses were paid for by the government. It was gracious of Governor Stubbs to officiate the inauguration ceremony at our humble village. This is a tribute of our sincere loyalty to the British Government, which has shown us great kindness. This plaque is specially erected in order not to forget this day.

Seventeen years later, the plaque would disappear when Japanese troops invaded and occupied Hong Kong. The official story is that the Japanese military authorities in Hong Kong had the plaque removed. However, given the fact that the inscription on the plaque contained a pledge of loyalty to the British, it would have been prudent for the villagers to have had the plaque quietly removed. Their allegiance to the British, blatantly cast in stone, would have become a dangerous political liability during the Japanese Occupation period.[26]

The general peace and prosperity enjoyed by Tang villagers in Kam Tin almost throughout the 20th century was only disrupted during the Japanese Occupation of Hong Kong that took place from January 1942 to August 1945. By the time hostilities broke out between Japan and the

Western powers, the British had already built a military base and an airfield right next to Kam Tin in Shek Kong. In other words, Kam Tin was sitting right next to a major target when the Japanese attacked Hong Kong. Older members of the Tang clan still vividly remember the time when Japanese troops arrived in Kam Tin. One such person was Tang Tim-kau (*Deng Tianqiu*), the village patriarch and former Village Representative of Shui Mei Tsuen, who told us his story:

> The Japanese soldiers came down the road and across the fields like a swarm of locusts. We sent our women and children to the forested hills to hide. Bridges spanning the road had been blown up by retreating British troops, but the Japanese got across anyway and kept advancing. When the Japanese entered our village, they asked for the village chief, who was my uncle. They did not molest us, but took over our ancestral hall and used it as headquarters for their officers. A few days later, they packed up and moved on. That was the last time we saw Japanese soldiers in such large numbers, as they were mostly stationed in the city.

On the whole, people living in the New Territories did not suffer as badly as those in the urban areas of Hong Kong because villagers could grow their own food and they lived a less material-dependent way of life. They were also much less subjected to harassment by soldiers of the Japanese occupation forces. The Japanese garrison in Hong Kong concentrated its effort on controlling the urban areas rather than spending valuable limited resources watching over villages.[27] In any case, there was no real need to maintain a large Japanese military presence in the New Territories, as villagers were cowed into submission by the draconian punitive measures of the Japanese military authorities. As James Hayes, a noted historian who served in the New Territories first as a District Officer and later as the Regional Secretary, writes:[28]

> The Japanese authorities reintroduced the principle of mutual responsibility . . . . This made leadership essential, and its practice potentially dangerous for the leaders. It obliged the village elders to organize themselves both to deal with the authorities and

with their own people, to meet the potential threat to themselves arising from misdemeanours, crime or anti-Japanese activity.

In fact, it was the Japanese authorities who introduced the now-familiar system of 'Village Representatives'. However, the Japanese had employed it as a sinister means to exercise social control by holding identifiable village leaders liable for the action of their fellow villagers.[29] After the war, the British retained the system as it provided District Officers who were tasked with the administration of the New Territories an expedient means of consulting with local village communities through elected representatives.

As the war dragged on, the economy of Hong Kong gradually degenerated into a state of near collapse, and food became increasingly expensive and scarce in the city areas. Villagers in the New Territories, however, were able to revert to subsistence farming and maintain a reasonable degree of self-sustenance. Nevertheless, life for the Tangs of Kam Tin had never been so hard since the Coastal Evacuation in the 1660s. As James Hayes summarizes, 'By the end of the [Japanese Occupation] period the New Territories' villagers were mostly in a desperate situation.'[30] When the British returned after VJ Day in 1945, the Tangs breathed a collective sigh of relief.

Notes

[1] Lord Salisbury in the House of Lords, 13 June 1898.
[2] Wordie, 2001, 12.
[3] See: Lockhart 1898, section 'Inhabitants', para. 6.
[4] See: Liu 1995, 26.
[5] *Hongkong Weekly Press*, vol. XLVIII, September 17, 1898, p. 139, quoted in Wesley-Smith 1973, 41.
[6] See: Liu 1995, 26.
[7] 'Journal of Inspection through the Newly Leased Territory', quoted in Wesley-Smith 1973, 41.
[8] *Hongkong Weekly Press*, vol. XLVIII, September 17, 1898, p. 139, quoted in Wesley-Smith 1973, 41.
[9] See: Lockhart 1900, 7.
[10] See: Kamm 1978, 212.
[11] See: Kamm 1978, 213.
[12] See: Lockhart 1900, 7.

[13] Authors' own translation from the Chinese text reproduced in Siu 1989, 85–86.
[14] See: Endacott 1973, 265.
[15] The reconstruction of the events leading to the Battle of Kam Tin is mainly based on Liu 1995, 46–50, 100–102 and Endacott 1973, 276.
[16] See: Liu 1995, 46.
[17] The single matshed and flagstaff can be seen in an historical photo of the flag-raising ceremony reproduced in Lau 1999, 24. In Lockhart 1900, 26 (under Appendix No. XIII), it is mentioned that 'the arrangement in connection with the hoisting of the flag on April 16th, which consisted in building a landing stage, forming an approach road, erecting of sheds, providing and erecting a flagstaff, etc., cost $2,085.00'.
[18] Founded in 1891 and disbanded in 1909, the Hong Kong Regiment was a unit whose troops were recruited from India for service in Hong Kong. It should not be confused with the Hong Kong Volunteers (also known by the full regimental title of the Hong Kong Artillery and Rifle Volunteer Corps in 1899), which adopted the name The Hong Kong Regiment in 1949.
[19] This was the proclamation containing an Order of the Queen's Council made on 20 October 1898. The proclamation is reproduced in Lockhart 1900, 29, under Appendix No. XX.
[20] Liu (1995,101–102) notes that the longstanding mistaken belief is based on the writings of Ding You in his book *Xiangang Chuqi Sihua* [an historical account of early Hong Kong] (Bejing: Joint Publishing (H.K.) Co., Ltd., 1958), which says that '. . . the British Army launched a counter-offensive, bombarded Kam Tin Wai [as Kat Hing Wai was sometimes referred to], and took away its iron gates as war trophy'. This account became the reference basis of many later writings on the gates of Kat Hing Wai.
[21] See: Wesley-Smith 1973, 42.
[22] Welsh 1993, 331–332.
[23] See: Lockhart 1900, 4.
[24] The Governor's speech originally published in *The Hong Kong Telegraph*, 27 May 1925; reproduced in Siu 1989, 87.
[25] The original Chinese text of the inscription is reproduced in Siu 1989, 85–86.
[26] This is purely the authors' speculation.
[27] The main Japanese garrison in the New Territories was stationed at Tai Po. Its key task was to monitor traffic flow in and out of the strategic town of Yuen Long.
[28] See: Hayes 1984, 59–60.
[29] See: Freedman 1976, 213.
[30] See: Hayes 1984, 59.

Fig. 18 Enormous festive signboards erected in the temple square in front of the Hung Shing Temple in celebration of the deity's birthday. *(Lee Ho Yin)*

CHAPTER THREE

Recent Past:
Kam Tin after World War II

From Farmland to Real Estate: The Decline of Agriculture in the New Territories

LIFE IN KAM TIN GRADUALLY RETURNED TO NORMAL after the war, and the Tangs quietly resumed their traditional agrarian way of life in their still fairly secluded environment, which was much as it had been since the Ming dynasty. But the outside world was changing rapidly and it would soon have a major effect on the economy, socio-politics, and physical environment of Kam Tin.

Like most places in the New Territories, the agricultural economy of Kam Tin had been centred on rice production. Following the civil war in China that culminated in the overthrow of the Kuomingtang (Nationalist) regime and the establishment of the Communist-led People's Republic of China, large numbers of refugees from mainland China settled in the New Territories. These immigrants had little means of livelihood other than farming. Suddenly, instead of toiling in the fields, landowners such as the Tangs were able to make a living by renting out their farmland to willing immigrants. Rice cultivation was a labour-intensive and time-consuming venture that yielded two crops annually. Immigrant farmers, who had to pay expensive rent for their fields, switched to more profitable vegetable farming which produced eight to ten crops per year.

In 1950, following the outbreak of the Korean War and direct military involvement of the newly established People's Republic of China in support of the North Korean forces, Western nations imposed a trade embargo on China. Hong Kong, as a British colony, had to be part of this trade sanction against mainland China. Because of the prevailing Cold War mentality, China was seen as a potential threat to the British Colony of Hong Kong. Under such circumstances, the Agricultural Department (which became the Agricultural and Fishery Department in 1953) began a policy to encourage vegetable farming, fish breeding, and livestock rearing, in order to reduce reliance on mainland China for the supply of vegetables and meat. The rapid increase in vegetable fields, fish ponds, and pig and poultry farms further contributed to the decline of the rice-production economy in the New Territories. The statistics are telling: in 1953, paddy fields in the New Territories consisted of 9,466 hectares, which was some 70% of the total farmland in Hong Kong. By 1988, less than one hectare of farmland was dedicated to rice cultivation.[1] Today, it is hard to believe that the New Territories was once a place where rice was cultivated in abundance. However, memories of rippling waves of ripening rice stalks swaying in the wind still survive in the minds of many elderly clanfolk.

The agricultural economy of the New Territories was further doomed when Hong Kong began industrialization in the 1950s, which had the effect of depleting manpower from labour-intensive farming activities. In the 1960s, sensing that there was no future in farming, the more educated younger generations of the clan villagers in the New Territories began to move to city areas to look for work, and a good number migrated overseas to seek jobs or set up business. By the mid-1970s, Britain alone had become the adopted home of some 10,000 clanfolk from the New Territories,[2] and there were many more in Australia and other Western European countries, such as Germany and Holland.

In the homes of many families we visited in Shui Tau Tsuen and Shui Mei Tsuen, we found photos displayed of sons and daughters posing before

Plate 1 Clanswomen in traditional work attire sitting outside the entrance of Kat Hing Wai. *(Lee Ho Yin)*

Plate 2 Farmland in Shui Tau Tsuen used for growing ornamental plants used in decorating homes during the Chinese New Year. *(Lee Ho Yin)*

Plate 3 Detail of an 1899 British map of Hong Kong that carries a note stating it was 'compiled from existing Intelligence Division maps of Hong Kong Admiralty Charts and a map of the Sun On District compiled in 1866 from the observation of an Italian Missionary'. Shui Tau Tsuen and Shui Mei Tsuen, located to the north of Kam-tin-hü, are marked as Pak-uk-tsün on the map. *(Public Records Office, Hong Kong)*

Plate 4 An aerial photo of Shui Tau Tsuen and Shui Mei Tsuen taken in 2000. *(Survey and Mapping Office, Hong Kong)*

Plate 5 Cheung Chun Yuen, an old martial arts school now used solely as an ancestral hall for Shui Tau Tsuen. *(Lynne Distefano)*

Plate 6 A small *ding dung* befitting the small ancestral altar in the minuscule building of Cheung Chun Yuen. *(Lee Ho Yin)*

Plate 7 The Earth God shrine at the village square of Shui Tau Tsuen. A small *ding dung* is hanging nearby. *(Lee Ho Yin)*

Plate 8 A large *ding dung*, or 'lantern of sons', in Shui Mei Tsuen's Tang Ching Lok Ancestral Hall during the Lantern Lighting Ceremony. *(Lee Ho Yin)*

Plate 9 Gigantic festive signboards decorating the Hung Shing Temple actually dwarf the little host building. *(Lee Ho Yin)*

Plate 10 Barbara Baker and Lynne DiStefano partake in Shui Mei Tsuen's annual communal feast to celebrate new sons born in the village in the previous year. *(Lee Ho Yin)*

Plate 11 Villagers happily carrying their prize of a 'floral shrine' while their village lion dances in celebration. *(Lee Ho Yin)*

Plate 12 Members of the lion-dancing team from the village of Tai Kong Po. During the annual festival of Shui Tau Tsuen and Shui Mei Tsuen, nearby villages send their lion-dancing teams to join in the celebration. *(Lee Ho Yin)*

Plate 13 Offerings of roast suckling pigs, cooked chicken, fruits, and incense made to the god Hung Shing on his birthday. *(Lee Ho Yin)*

Plate 14 A Cantonese-pop singer performing to a packed temple square during the annual twin-festival to celebrate the birthday of god Hung Shing in Shui Tau Tsuen and the birth of new sons in Shui Mei Tsuen. *(Lee Ho Yin)*

Plate 15 The doorway of one of the few remaining traditional houses in Shui Tau Tsuen. Most of such houses are no longer inhabited—they are either abandoned or used for storage. *(Lynne DiStefano)*

Fig. 19 Vegetable fields at the outskirts of Shui Tau Tsuen. They represent some of the last remaining cultivated farmland in the area. *(Lee Ho Yin)*

streetscapes and landscapes in the West. The answers to our enquiry were always the same: no, they were not holiday snapshots, but photos sent back by children who had migrated to the West. Tang Tim-kau (*Deng Tianqiu*), the village patriarch of Shui Mei Tsuen, was a typical case. His house was decorated with souvenirs brought from Australia when he visited his fifth son, who had been settled there for some thirty years. The old Tang was the last in his family to have farmed for a living; his eldest son, Johnny Tang, had succeeded him as the village representative, and his other children were now successful professionals working in the city. When asked why his children did not continue the farming tradition, he answered, with a typical tone of Cantonese practicality, that farming was extremely hard work, and it was not a good way for his children to make a living, especially when they had the education and the means to pursue better careers.

The Small House Policy: The Shape of Villages to Come

LIKE MANY HONGKONGERS, we have come to take for granted the semi-urbanized 'rural' landscape in the New Territories, the physical environment of which is dominated by modern flat-roofed village houses that are uniformly three stories high and constructed of reinforced concrete. Yet, as recently as thirty years ago, Shui Tau Tsuen and Shui Mei Tsuen, like other villages in the New Territories, homogeneously consisted of traditional Southern-Chinese style village houses with mud- or clay-brick walls and tiled roofs. Many such village houses dated back to the Qing dynasty (1616–1911), and some even to the Ming dynasty (1368–1644). They were repaired and rebuilt over the centuries using long-established construction materials, techniques, and aesthetic principals. It was because of this persistence of traditional architectonics that the villages were able to retain the consistent physical character that typified Chinese villages in the New Territories for so many centuries. The first post-war edition (1946) of the *Annual Report on Hong Kong* depicts what villages were like before they succumbed to modern development:[3]

Fig. 20 A large fishpond owned by a family from Shui Mei Tsuen, now being leased for recreational fishing. *(Lee Ho Yin)*

> Village houses in the New Territories . . . are usually built of locally made blue brick [also referred to as grey brick] or cut granite with a tiled roof and cement floor though some of the poorer type are built of sun-dried mud-brick faced with plaster. A typical village dwelling consists of one ground floor room, entrance being made through the front door—there is no back door—into a partially roofed over space, one side of which is reserved for cooking, and the other side for storage of dried grass, the principal fuel. An inner door gives entrance to the single room, the rear portion of which is screened off with wooden partitions for use as a bedroom. Over this rear portion, raised some 8 feet above floor level, is a wooden platform or gallery known as the 'cockloft', which is used for storage purposes or for extra sleeping accommodation if the family is large. The house has no ceiling, except the rafters and tiles, and no chimney. Windows are rare.

Fig. 21 Traditional grey-brick houses of Shui Mei Tsuen around the mid-1970s. These represented the typical kind of domestic village architecture in the New Territories before the Small House Policy took hold. *(Information Services Department, Hong Kong)*

> Dwellings are sometimes built in rows of a dozen or so in the larger villages, with the front row facing the back of another row; whilst at other times they are built haphazard to conform with 'Fung Shui' . . . , a form of Chinese necromancy which traditionally governs the siting of dwellings and graves. The streets between the dwellings are usually not more than six to eight feet wide, and the drainage is primitive. Lavatories are erected apart from the dwellings, and are similar, though inferior, to those still found attached to some rural cottages in the United Kingdom. The houses are for the most part kept in reasonable repair and the structural design is never altered. Furnishings consist usually of trestle beds, perhaps a table, and a few small stools.

The above quotation would accurately describe a typical village setting in the New Territories during the Ming and Qing dynasties. In fact, up to the 1960s, so few changes had been made to the physical aspects of villages that scenes of the New Territories were virtually indistinguishable from those portrayed in 19th century photographs. This traditional New Territories setting began to unravel rapidly in the 1960s when development in the urban areas on Hong Kong Island and Kowloon Peninsula could not cope with the rising urban population and growing manufacturing industry. This prompted the government to look into land resources in the rural New Territories, which consequently led to the resumption of large tracts of farmland. That was when the sensitive issue of ownership and development rights of village land came to a head.

The issue of land ownership had been the main contention between the clans and the government since the New Territories became incorporated into the British colony in 1898. The transfer to British rule was initially resisted by the Tang clan—the biggest collective landowner in the New Territories—out of fear that their land would be taken away. From a strictly technical sense, the British colonial government did take away their land. After the British took over the New Territories, the status of privately owned land was transformed from freehold to leasehold, which required the payment of an annual Crown rent to the government. However, the change of legal status in the nature of land ownership did not

change the status quo in practice, as villagers retained the use of the land with little administrative interference. To the villagers, it was indiscernible from owning their land and paying land taxes to the local government, which was the way it had been for centuries. Hence, there was no complaint. Furthermore, as the economy of the New Territories was based on farming and little else, land was worth little in itself, other than how much harvest it could bring to farmers. There was no business potential in property development on village land, as restrictive measures had been imposed to prevent speculative developers from exploiting cheap land in the New Territories.

All was relatively well until the 1960s, when the government began to draft plans to develop New Towns—self-sustainable mini cities with local industries—in the hitherto untouched New Territories areas. By this time, the agricultural-based economy in the New Territories was already sliding towards terminal decline. As the government began to resume land for infrastructural, housing, and industrial development needs, suddenly land in the New Territories was no longer valued according to what could be grown from it but according to what could be built on it. Disputes immediately arose over the government's compensation rates for resumed farmland and village properties, which villagers considered to be under market value. Villagers were also dissatisfied with statutory restrictions imposed on the sale and development of village properties, which they saw as unjust measures that deprived them of a share of the emerging land-economics pie baked in their own front yard.

At this point, the full implication of the leasehold status of village land became manifest. The clans realized that they were losing out in the economic dividend. They unleashed their powerful political representative body, Heung Yee Kuk (which literally means 'village affairs office'), to pressure the government for a fairer deal. For Heung Yee Kuk, it was a role for which it was originally set up some forty years previously. In 1924, clan leaders in the New Territories formed a voluntary organization to pressure the government against a policy that levied premiums on permanent structures built on agricultural land.[4] What started off as a pressure group, that is, an 'NGO' in today's terminology, which the government had failed in several attempts to outlaw, was to become a government-recognized political representative body for villagers in the New Territories in 1959.

Fig. 22 Caught between a rock and a hard place—a traditional village house between a demolished neighbour and a row of modern 'Spanish-style villas'. *(Lee Ho Yin)*

To cut a long and complicated story short, after protracted negotiations with Heung Yee Kuk, the Hong Kong Government relented and introduced the 'Small House Policy'.[5] Under the policy, qualified villagers who possess private village land may apply for a once-in-a-lifetime licence at no premium to build a 'small house', more commonly known as *ding uk* (literally, 'son's house'), of a specified height and floor area. If the villagers have no land of their own on which to build small houses, they can apply for a plot of government land at a concessionary premium—two-thirds of the market value. Villagers also retain the right to transfer ownership of their small houses. Currently, the specifications for a New Territories small house is a three-storey residential building not exceeding 27 feet (8.23 metres) in height and with a footprint area of not more than 700 square feet (65.03 square metres).[6] Essentially, the policy is designed to serve the dual purpose of preventing rampant property development in the New Territories while keeping villagers happy by allowing them to build

Fig. 23 A cluster of 'small houses' built on farmland and overlooking a disused fishpond in Shui Mei Tsuen. Such three-storey reinforced concrete buildings built to the specifications of the Small House Policy have become the typical modern village house found in the New Territories today. *(Lee Ho Yin)*

bigger houses. In the event, what seems impeccable in theory rarely works the way it is intended in practice.

As the Small House Policy was introduced, it was necessary to spell out who exactly were the eligible candidates. When the New Territories was transferred to British administration in 1898 the clans organized military resistance against the British. Fearing the prospect of ruling a hostile population, the British pacified the angry clans by promising to respect their traditions and preserve their customary rights. Hence, in keeping with the patrilineal tradition of the clans, the government declared that the policy extended only to those classified as 'indigenous villagers', which refers to men of at least 18 years of age who are 'descended through the male line from a resident in 1898 of a recognized village'.[7] By such a definition, the Small House Policy is essentially limited to male members of the New Territories clans whose legally acceptable proof of their 'indigenous' status can be obtained from meticulously maintained genealogical records and ancestral gravestones. Through the Small House Policy, village clansmen in the New Territories acquired legal status of their collective identity, and they would exploit it as lawful justification to

maintain their traditional rights in post-colonial Hong Kong. This was to become the root cause of a number of social, political, and land economics issues that would haunt the Hong Kong Special Administrative Region Government.

Today, the Small House Policy is seen as a colonial legacy that has stratified the New Territories society into the privileged indigenous villagers and those who are deemed non-indigenous. The sentiment was summed up by Lau Siu-kai, associate director of the Chinese University's Institute of Asia-Pacific Studies: 'Politically, it is increasingly unacceptable [for indigenous villagers to retain such rights after the Handover], but historically it is justifiable'.[8] A bigger issue that has surfaced is the inherently gender-discriminatory nature of the Small House Policy, which, miraculously, is exempted from the 1995 Sex Discrimination Ordinance.

The fact that a blatantly discriminatory policy is able to coexist legally with an anti-discrimination ordinance is demonstrative of the political influence of Heung Yee Kuk on the government and the legislature. In 1999, the Equal Opportunities Commission proposed to revoke the exemption of the Small House Policy from the Sex Discrimination Ordinance, but the proposal was voted down by the Legislative Council. Again, Heung Yee Kuk saw the action as a threat against the traditional rights of indigenous villagers, which had been guaranteed by the colonial government and enshrined in the Basic Law, Hong Kong's post-colonial mini-constitution. However, as former legislator and women's rights activist Cyd Ho pointed out, the supposed right to build small houses was never an age-old custom, but an administrative policy implemented under the circumstances of the New Territories in the 1970s.[9]

Many indigenous villagers have exploited the Small House Policy and benefited from it financially, for no one had predicted the boom in Hong Kong's property market that took off in the late 1970s. As a result, many indigenous village families were able to reap huge financial gain by selling off their sons' small houses or permits to build small houses. The government recognized the commercial exploitation of small houses as early as 1978, and tried to plug the loophole by requiring the payment of premium at full market value in the sale of small houses.[10] However, such a measure was soon rendered ineffectual by the insatiable market demand for properties in the New Territories.

Fig. 24 The impact of the Small House Policy on the physical setting of villages in the New Territories is aptly expressed in this photo that shows a modern 'Spanish-style villa' rising from the ruins of a traditional village house in Shui Tau Tsuen. *(Lee Ho Yin)*

As property prices in the New Territories soared through the 1980s and 1990s, the sale of small houses became a hugely profitable business. A small house today costs about a million Hong Kong dollars to build, and can be sold for around four to six million dollars! Alternatively, the three-storey house can be rented out at a monthly rate of about four thousand dollars per floor. However, the most lucrative means of commercial exploitation of small houses is to sell them even before they are built. As local journalist Kevin Sinclair explained, 'It is a racket which has turned into an industry. As soon as a boy reaches 18, he can "sell" his name and address to a developer. The going price . . . is now [HK]$300,000.'[11]

The biggest contention of the Small House Policy, however, is the way it has destroyed the rural landscape of the New Territories. In maximizing the sale value of small houses, indigenous villagers all have their small houses built to the permitted building height and gross floor area. Since such houses do not require the usual building approval process, there is no need for the service of professional architects, and they are often built to the standard designs provided by contractors. Needless to say, the architectural result is one of unimaginative uniformity. Towards the late 1980s, as small houses became more prevalent, some contractors began to engage the help of freelance architects or even design students to provide design input to small houses in order to boost sales.[12] As it was necessary to maximize property value by building to the maximum allowable height and floor area, designers had little room for creative input except to decorate the standard concrete box as best as they could.

The 1980s was a time when Post-Modernism ruled the aesthetic trend in architecture, and local architects were keen to copy the superficial aspects of Western Classicism. Many small houses produced during this period were poor imitations of southern European houses along the Mediterranean coast. For inexplicable reasons, the public related such pseudo-Mediterranean architectural aesthetics to the vernacular architecture of southern Spain, and small houses have ever since been commonly referred to as 'Spanish-style villas'. The road from traditional Chinese houses to modern Spanish-style villas is akin to a comedy of errors. But it is hard to appreciate the funny side of things when one sees how the New Territories have turned into a country of concrete boxes decorated in Post-Modern Mediterranean kitsch.

Breaking the Political Monopoly: Women's Rights and Voting Rights of Non-indigenous Villagers

AT THE END OF THE 20TH CENTURY, there was a general premonition that the history of Kam Tin as a traditional village society might have unfolded its final chapter. In the early 1990s, rumblings were heard about the discriminatory nature of the patriarchal social system of New Territories clans, in which only men had the right to inherit land and properties. The rumbles turned into a storm when supporters of women's rights clashed with conservative clansmen who saw their traditional patrilineal rights and power being challenged and eroded. However, the times were changing, and discriminatory traditions guarded by a zealous minority had to relent in the face of modern ideals supported by an overwhelming majority. In June 1994, a law was passed to grant inheritance rights to women

Fig. 25 The *ding dung* hung in the main hall of Tang Ching Lok Ancestral Hall. *(Lee Ho Yin)*

clanfolk in the New Territories. Strangely, when we spoke with Tang clansmen in Shui Tau Tsuen and Shui Mei Tsuen, few of them objected to this law. As one clansman put it, 'Aww, men or women, we belong to the same clan'. We wondered why, given the ferocity of the protests staged by New Territories clanfolk back in early 1994. Then it dawned upon us that the Tang clan of Kam Tin, unlike other clans in the New Territories, had set a unique and unprecedented tradition of honouring a woman—the famous Wong Ku, the lost Song princess—on the all-male ancestral altar.

Today, despite traditional strong biases against women in the patriarchal clan society in the New Territories, there are 13 female Village Representatives (elected village leaders) among the 600-plus villages in Hong Kong.[13] The number of female village chiefs is still too few, and there are none in Kam Tin, but the trend for greater socio-political rights for clanswomen has been set. In 1999, we were invited to attend the 'Lantern Lighting Ceremony' in the ancestral hall of Shui Mei Tsuen, which celebrated the birth of sons in the village during the previous year. The significance of this ceremony is rooted in the patriarchal nature of New Territories clan villages, in which financial and social status are invested along the male line.

As we sat at a table enjoying the communal feast of delicacies and special rice porridge that were served to mark the occasion, a middle-aged clanswoman beside us recalled that the feast used to be an exclusively male affair. 'In my childhood days, only men were allowed to partake in the feast in the ancestral hall, while women had to leave after paying respect to the ancestors.' Raising her voice purposefully, she continued, 'But now, even I can sit with the men in the ancestral hall.' A clansman about her age, sitting across the table, busying himself with a mouthful of food, nodded in agreement, echoing her words, 'Yeah, it really doesn't matter now; women should have the same rights as men.' A hint of a contented smile came to her face as she slurped the hot porridge brought to her respectfully by a younger clansman.

Fig. 26 Ancestral tablets used for the worship of male ancestors laid out for repainting in an ancestral hall in Shui Tau Tsuen. *(Lee Ho Yin)*

Besides admitting women into the village political system, Kam Tin may face another challenge for greater political rights from village residents who are not classified under the status of 'indigenous villager'. This issue arose out of a landmark court case in 1999, when an angry fish farmer by the name of Chan Wah took the government to court to challenge the election system for Village Representatives in the New Territories, which restricted eligible voters to indigenous villagers. Although Chan was born in his resident village of Po Toi O and was married to an indigenous villager, he was denied the right to vote because he was a non-indigenous villager. His representing lawyer, Barrister Philip Dykes S.C., branded the existing election system a 'legal museum' based on a colonial government policy to maintain the socio-political status quo, which served to pacify the hostile clans, when the British took over the New Territories in 1898.[14] The case was pursued all the way to the Court of Final Appeal (Hong Kong Special Administrative Region's highest court), which delivered the final

Fig. 27 Male and female villagers sharing the same table in the annual communal feast held in the ancestral hall of Shui Mei Tsuen. Despite the thriving patriarchal social system in New Territories' villages, the privilege of partaking in communal feasts is no longer exclusive to clansmen. *(Lee Ho Yin)*

ruling on 22 December 2000, declaring that the election system was discriminatory and unlawful. The ruling made headlines in all local papers on the following day. As reported in the *South China Morning Post*,[15] the five judges of the Court of Final Appeal had unanimously ruled that

> . . . because the system only recognized indigenous villagers—those who could trace their ancestry to pre-colonial times—it breached the Bill of Rights and Sex Discrimination Ordinance. It was unreasonable to deny non-indigenous villagers the right to vote or stand as a candidate.

After the court ruling, members of Heung Yee Kuk, the political representative body for indigenous villagers in the New Territories, bitterly argued with the government and among themselves over a controversial government proposal to have two Village Representatives for each village—one elected by indigenous villagers and the other by all residents, including non-indigenous villagers.[16] No matter how strong the resistance is among conservative members of Heung Yee Kuk, they are fighting a losing battle to preserve the political monopoly that had been expediently preserved by the British colonial authorities. This is especially so when post-colonial Hong Kong is becoming an increasingly cosmopolitan society in which discriminatory practices are no longer tolerated by the vast majority.

The socio-political repercussions of this court ruling for Kam Tin are that Kam Tin may see a non-Chinese Village Representative elected to one of its villages in the near future. Kam Tin now has the largest concentration of people of Nepalese descent in the whole of Hong Kong. These Nepalese Hongkongers are descendants of Gurkha soldiers who were once based in the nearby Shek Kong Camp (now taken over by the aviation unit of the Hong Kong garrison of the People's Liberation Army). In the early 1980s, following the successful conclusion of Sino–British talks about the future of Hong Kong after 1997, the British military no longer had a role to play in Hong Kong. Gurkha units that were based in Hong Kong were gradually disbanded or redeployed elsewhere. Many of the Nepalese servicemen who had been stationed in Hong Kong for a long time had brought their families over. As a result, many of their children became permanent residents of Hong Kong either by birth or by having

Fig. 28 A Nepalese woman at the gateway of Tai Hong Wai, a walled village with a majority Nepalese population. Kam Tin today has the biggest concentration of Nepalese people, a legacy of the Gurkha military training centre once based in the nearby Shek Kong Camp.
(Lee Ho Yin)

fulfilled the seven-year-stay requirement. Today, there are about 2,000 of them living in 13 villages, and the walled village of Tai Hong Wai is the adopted home of some 700 Nepalese residents, who represent about 80% of the village population. One of its residents, Roshan Limbu, an outspoken young man born to a former Gurkha soldier, publicly announced his ambition to become the first Nepalese to be elected village head.[17]

Hung Shing and Ding Dung: The Persistence of Village Cultural Traditions

WHEN WE FIRST MET TANG TIM-KAU (*Deng Tianqiu*) in 1998, he was still the Village Representative of Shui Mei Tsuen. We queried him about the cultural traditions of the two villages. Avoiding our difficult-to-answer questions in the typical indirect way, he mused, 'People keep asking me these questions. Just the other day, someone from the local museum came and asked me the same thing.' Just as we thought we would be going away empty handed, he proposed, 'As I told that museum person, why don't you come to our annual village festival early next year and see for yourself? I'm giving you an invitation.' It was to be held on the 15th day of the first lunar month—the last day of the traditional Chinese New Year celebration period. It would be the one single event that would explain the essence of the cultural traditions of the two villages, as the old Tang clansman promised.

The day arrived and we returned to Shui Tau Tsuen and Shui Mei Tsuen. As we neared the villages, we could hear the familiar heavy drumbeat of lion dancing interspersed with the crackling noise of exploding firecrackers. Although firecrackers have been banned in Hong Kong, their use in village festivals is tolerated by the police. The car park area at the entrance of Shui Tau Tsuen was packed with cars. A volunteer car-park marshal was busy directing vehicles bringing in guests and visitors. Teams of lion dancers from neighbouring villages arrived in pickup trucks that were decorated with colourful ensigns of their respective pugilistic clubs. Television news teams arrived with their over-sized video cameras, as did droves of amateur photographers carrying bulging camera bags. Everyone seemed to be guided by the din of drumbeat and firecrackers and to be drawn towards a place deep in the villages where something big was happening.

When we arrived at the centre of the noise and human traffic, we were impressed by the sheer spectacle of the sight. The festival was taking place in the villages' main temple square, which is strategically located at the boundary between the two villages. Gigantic three-storey high temporary billboards constructed of red paper mounted over bamboo frames lined the walls around the square. Such huge placards, sponsored by well-wishing individuals and groups, are the traditional means of announcing a celebratory event. They are also an indirect way of showing off the well-wishers' wealth (by sponsoring the biggest and most elaborately decorated billboard) and status (by displaying the sponsors' honours and businesses). The sound of a woman singing a Cantonese pop song blared from loudspeakers rigged to bamboo poles. This came from a singer performing on a temporary bamboo stage facing the temple at the opposite

Fig. 29 Clansmen enjoying a feast of traditional delicacies and modern-day beer in the customary way—by standing around the table as they eat and drink. *(Lee Ho Yin)*

Fig. 30 A Cantonese-pop singer on a temporary stage performing to a lone audience in Shui Tau Tsuen's temple square. In the past, Cantonese opera rather than modern pop-songs were the norm. *(Lee Ho Yin)*

Fig. 31 A lion dances in front of Tang Ching Lok Ancestral Hall after having gone into the building to pay respect to the Tang ancestors. *(Lee Ho Yin)*

Fig. 32 When lion-dancing teams from two pugilistic clubs meet, a ritual battle between the lions ensures. The village festival provides a public venue for lion-dancing teams to competitively demonstrate their skills. *(Lee Ho Yin)*

Fig. 33 The object of celebration for Shui Mei Tsuen's annual festival—sons born into the village in the previous year. In New Territories villages, sons are as important for their small-house building rights in today's money-driven land economy as they were in the days of a labour-intensive agricultural economy. *(Lee Ho Yin)*

Fig. 34 A large *ding dung*, or 'lantern of sons', hanging from a roof beam in the main hall of Tang Ching Lok Ancestral Hall. Smaller lanterns are also placed at the villages' Earth God shrines and at the altar of Hung Shing Temple *(Lee Ho Yin)*

end of the square. The performance was really meant for the god housed in the temple, and not for the mortal beings gate-crashing his birthday party. In the past, a traditional Cantonese opera troupe would have occupied the stage, but it has become increasingly common to hire modern Canto-pop bands instead.

The festival was actually a double celebration shared by both Shui Tau Tsuen and Shui Mei Tsuen. For the villagers of Shi Tau Tsuen, they were hosting the celebration of the birthday of deity Hung Shing. Among the many legends of Hung Shing, the most common one tells of his mortal origin as a righteous prefecture governor and an amateur meteorologist in the Tang dynasty. He became rather good at his pastime and often provided fisherfolk with accurate weather forecasts, which probably created the myth that he could control the weather. When he died, apparently of overwork, he was promptly deified and worshipped as a god. Being a weather god, he was, and still is, worshipped by fisherfolk and farmers alike in Hong Kong. Temples dedicated to Hung Shing are common in Hong Kong. The one in Shui Tau Tsuen is a small Ming dynasty building that began life as a humble little shrine.

As we stood outside the temple trying to take in everything and make sense of it, devotees flowed into the building bearing offerings of food and ritual-papers. Suddenly, the drumbeat quickened in rhythm and increased decibels. It was the auspicious moment to deliver birthday wishes to Hung Shing. Teams of lion dancers flowed into the temple square and took turns to perform an energetic ritual dance at the temple entrance before they went inside the building to kowtow before the statue of the birthday god on the altar. It was surreal to see so many make-believe Chinese lions diligently play their part in paying respect to a mythical being. The performance, although carried out explicitly for religious reasons, also carried an implicit secular motive. It was an undeclared competition among the many lion dancing teams to show off the pugilistic skills embodied in the disciplines of lion dancing. The drummers, drenched in sweat, hammered away with locked brows and determined expressions on their faces, not unlike the look of warriors in the heat of battle. We began to appreciate the military-like intensity displayed by these lion-dancers as we remembered that the village clubs they represented were the present-day incarnation of village vigilante groups.

Propped against the front wall of the temple were a dozen curious looking structures that resembled towers made of paper. They were large, about a metre wide and three metres tall, but they were light and delicate, as was made apparent by the careful yet effortless way two men had lifted them into place. Gaudily decorated with colourful paper flowers and small clay figures depicting famous characters from history and mythology, these are constructions of paper over a framework of bamboo splits and are known as 'floral shrines'. In the past, these shrines were prizes to be won in a game played by competing teams from the various village pugilistic clubs. The game, called the 'floral-shrine scramble', was simple: competing teams only had to snatch a ball of red cloth containing a number, which was fired into the air with gunpowder. Each floral shrine corresponded to a number, and the ones with the auspicious numbers were the most eagerly, and often literally, fought over, which led to the banning of the game by police in recent years. These days, the floral shrines are won by a more civil, but much less fun, game of lottery instead.

Fig. 35 Villagers happily carrying off the floral shrine they have won while their village lion dances in celebration. *(Lee Ho Yin)*

Fig. 36 Village elders in formal traditional gowns preparing to carry out the lottery draw for the various floral-shrine prizes. The wooden bucket contains numbered discs corresponding to various floral shrines. 'Minders' in sunglasses are deployed to ensure orderliness during the lottery draw. *(Lee Ho Yin)*

Fig. 37 A sumptuous offering of roasted suckling pigs laid out before the altar of Hung Shing in the smoky temple, where incense and ritual papers are burnt in abundance in honour of the god's birthday. *(Lynne DiStefano)*

Fig. 38 Villagers in front of floral shrines. *(Lee Ho Yin)*

Fig. 39 A Cantonese-pop singer and village children performing for a large audience on a temporary bamboo stage erected in the temple square facing the Hung Shing Temple. Today, it is not uncommon to have Cantonese-pop shows instead of traditional Cantonese opera performed at village festivals. *(Lee Ho Yin)*

Fig. 40 The statue of Hung Shing in his namesake's temple in Shui Tau Tsuen. Hung Shing, a god of weather and the patron deity of Hong Kong farming and fishing communities, is peculiar to Hong Kong. *(Information Services Department, Hong Kong)*

Fig. 41 Lion-dancers and drummers play out their dance routine with intense ferocity, as shown in the facial expression of this lion-dancer from the Kat Hing Wai lion-dancing team. *(Lee Ho Yin)*

Fig. 42 The villagers of Shui Tau Tsuen and Shui Mei Tsuen celebrating the annual village festival in the temple square. *(Lee Ho Yin)*

With the floral shrines in place, a couple of village elders dressed in their traditional best mounted a table placed in the middle of the temple square to get ready to officiate the floral-shrine lottery. But, for us, it was time to leave the increasing clamour of the excited crowd to look for Chief Tang. We went into the Tang Ching Lok Ancestral Hall, located next to the temple, where another celebration was taking place. The ancestral hall, also a Ming dynasty building, was built to commemorate the namesake Tang ancestor, who belonged to the 17th generation Tang clan in Kam Tin. As we walked through the entrance, the last of the dancing lions to come to pay respect to the ancestors was finishing its routine. Displayed in the central hall of the building were several enormous lanterns hanging from the roof beams. These were objects of celebration for Shui Mei Tsuen. Called *ding dung* in Cantonese, which means 'lanterns of sons', they were made for the annual ceremony of *dim ding dung*, or 'lighting the lanterns of sons', to celebrate sons born into the village in the previous year.

Only families that have been blessed with male newborns are given the privilege of lighting such lanterns and partaking in a special feast held in this ancestral temple. Although it may be discriminatory in today's politically correct environment, sons were once vital to the agrarian communities in the New Territories, as they formed the basis of manpower for farming work and patrilineal succession to land and properties. Of course, as discussed earlier, sons have taken an even greater economic role for families of indigenous villagers in the New Territories, as they have acquired the special right to develop highly profitable properties under the Small House Policy.

The courtyards and halls were already filled with tables and chairs set up for the banquet. The ancestors being worshipped on the altars in the sacred end hall were also given their share of the feast in the form of offerings of cups of rice wine and a roasted suckling pig. We spotted Chief Tang at the head table, and he immediately came over to usher us to one of the guest tables. He was beaming as he said, 'You see, isn't it better to come and see what our cultural traditions are all about instead of having me explain them?' We could not agree more.

The End of Village Tradition: The Future of Shui Tau Tsuen and Shui Mei Tsuen

WHILE THE DOUBLE-CELEBRATION CONTINUES every year in Shui Tau Tsuen and Shui Mei Tsuen, the temporary joy of the villagers is overshadowed by a looming development that will put an end to their traditional village society. In November 1997, the Kowloon–Canton Railway Corporation (KCRC) announced the HK$51.7 billion West Rail Project that will span a 30.5 km rail line across the western part of the New Territories.[18] At the time when this book was written, phase I of KCRC's West Rail Project, which began in October 1998, was well underway. When the project is completed at the end of 2003, Kam Tin will become one of the designated stops along the West Rail network. With the West Rail in place, Kam Tin will be ready to proceed with what government planners have envisioned for it—the development of a New Town that will eventually accommodate up to 1.5 million people. The centre of this future New Town will be built around the new train station, which is located within walking distance of the villages of Shui Mei and Shui Tau. When this happens, the villages of Shui Mei and Shui Tau, along with other villages in their vicinity, will be swallowed up by urban development. Kam Tin will surely cease to be a clan-based multi-village community, and will be reincarnated as a modern urban centre.

Three years after the announcement of the West Rail Project, on one of our visits to Shui Tau Tsuen and Shui Mei Tsuen, we asked some of the villagers how they felt about the project and its implications. All of them simply accepted the impending fate of their villages with a fatalistic shrug. Their unspoken resignation was plain on their faces. The fate of their villages had been sealed as huge railway viaducts loomed incongruously against the distant mountains that surrounded the plains of Kam Tin. However, one particular villager offered a glimmer of optimism as he boldly predicted that the Tang clan of Kam Tin would adapt to the new changes just as it had survived wars and turmoil in the past. 'Our ancestors are buried in places with great feng-shui,' he explained, 'and the changes may bring even greater prosperity to our clan.'

Notes

[1] See: Lau 1999, 125.
[2] See: Lau 1999, 129.
[3] See: *Annual Report on Hong Kong for the Year 1946*, 1947, 55.
[4] See: Lee 1984, 164.
[5] This policy was the brainchild of Denis Bray, the then New Territories District Commissioner, who still lives in Hong Kong.
[6] This means that the maximum allowable floor area for a small house is 3 storeys x 700 square feet = 2,100 square feet (195.09 square metres). To put it in a monetary perspective, the square-footage price for a small house in 2001 was about HK$2,000, which means that a small house may be worth around HK$4.2 million.
[7] The definition is given in the pamphlet 'The New Territories Small House Policy: How to Apply for a Small House' issued by the Lands Department, September 1997 (downloadable from the government website: http://www.info.gov.hk/landsd/public/house/house./htm).
[8] See: Li 1999, 2.
[9] See: Ng 2001, 14.

[10] See: Lau 1999, 110–111.
[11] See: Sinclair 1999, 2.
[12] One of the authors of this book, who used to work as an architect, was once involved in a project to design a village small house for a contractor.
[13] See: *Sunday Morning Post* article by Lai (18 July 1999, 3).
[14] See: Buddle 1999, 6.
[15] See: Mo 2000, 1.
[16] See: Chan 2001, 11; Lau 2001, 22.
[17] See: Lee 2001, 1.
[18] All figures relating to the West Rail Project are obtained from information released on the Internet by the KCRC and Government Information Centre.

Fig. 43 Mr. Tang Tim-kau, Village Representative of Shui Mei Tsuen from 1967 to 1999. *(Lee Ho Yin)*

CHAPTER FOUR

Village Voice:
The World According to the Tangs

Traditional Past to Modern Present

AS IN MOST VILLAGES IN THE NEW TERRITORIES, the buildings in Shui Tau Tsuen and Shui Mei Tsuen are mostly of the ubiquitous 'Spanish-style villa' variety, which are, in our opinion, rather unattractive but pragmatic modern houses. Since the villages have always been practical living habitats for the residents rather than romantic showpieces for tourists, there is little incentive for the villagers to preserve their former traditional setting. What little remains of the traditional architectural fabric is frequently vacant, and, in many cases, left to decay. Concrete is everywhere: on the ground as well as on the walls. However, the original social fabric of the two villages is largely intact. The villages are still mainly populated by the original Tangs, and most of the old and modern village houses are still lived in by families of the villages' own native sons rather than sold or rented to outsiders. Despite having lost much of their physical charm as a result of the Small House Policy, the villages are, nevertheless, worthy of a visit,

Fig. 44 An Earth God shrine in the corner of the village square of Shui Tau Tsuen. *(Lee Ho Yin)*

and the industrious visitor will still see vestiges of beauty as well as items of interest.

When we first entered Shui Tau Tsuen, we thought we had walked into the village car park, but it turned out it was not what it seemed. The realization came when we spotted remains of what the space used to be like as we looked around the hoards of randomly parked cars. A shrine for the village's Earth God stood at one corner, and near to it was a disused communal well, which had been sealed over with a rusty metal mesh screen. Near the centre of the space was a banyan tree—the village's feng-shui tree—under which huddled four old ladies engrossed in a game of fan-tan. These were faint reminders of a former village square, where bare-footed children used to run about in play, bare-chested clansmen squatted and smoked large bamboo pipes, and women wearing wide-brimmed hats gossiped as they drew water from the communal well.

Shui Tau Tsuen is the bigger of the two villages and has about 600 *men* living in 200-plus households. The village elder who quoted us the men-only population figure grinned apologetically as he explained that it was customary to only consider men as village members, while women born or married into the village clan were not counted. A number of the clansmen included in the census have actually migrated overseas, but they are counted anyway as they are still formally registered as residents of

Fig. 45 A disused village well, covered with a rusty metal mesh screen in Shui Tau Tsuen. The availability of clean piped water in every village home has rendered the drawing of water from wells an obsolete task.
(Lee Ho Yin)

Fig. 46 The physical environment of Shui Tau Tsuen and Shui Mei Tsuen today—modern three-storey 'Spanish-style villas' interspersed with traditional village houses that are often vacant and left to decay. *(Lee Ho Yin)*

112 A TALE OF TWO VILLAGES

Fig. 47 One of the four younger brothers of Mr. Johnny Tang, the incumbent Village Representative of Shui Mei Tsuen, cooks over a traditional brick stove in the kitchen of his parents' old house.
(Lee Ho Yin)

the village. We asked exactly how many absentee villagers there were, but the village elder either could not or would not tell us, and we had to leave it at that. We bumped into Johnny Tang, the incumbent Village Representative of Shui Mei Tsuen, in front of the Hung Shing Temple that stands between Shui Tau Tsuen and Shui Mei Tsuen. We raised our question about the two villages' populations. He was more forthcoming with the figures, 'What you've been told about Shui Tau Tsuen sounds about right.' He made a mental calculation and told us that Shui Mei Tsuen has about 200 men, of whom only about 100 actually live in the village in around 60 to 70 households.[1] But what was life like in the villages before they became what they are today?

The Young Village Representative's Story

JOHNNY TANG REPRESENTS THE NEW GENERATION of village leaders. In his early fifties, he is considered a young man for the job. He took over the post of village head from his father in 1999, when Tang senior decided that he was too old to run again for office. This seemed just like the traditional practice in imperial China, where it was natural for sons to succeed fathers in jobs ranging from the mightiest emperors and generals to the most humble farmers and manual labourers. But it was not the case with Johnny—he was nominated and elected to the post by fellow villagers in the last Village Representative election. Johnny chose to carry on his father's public service practically by default. Being the eldest son, he had to assist his father to carry out the duties of a Village Representative, and he had acquired a wealth of wisdom and experience in the process. He was therefore seen as the most competent person for the job. We asked what he could remember from his childhood days, and this was his story:

> I remember my grandfather telling me that in his younger days there were bandits roaming about, which is why there are so

many fortified walled villages in Kam Tin. There used to be a fortified village here as well, and it was called Pak Wai [literally 'north wall']. It was meant as a sanctuary for the people of the two villages in the event of a bandit raid, but there were fewer incidents of banditry after the British came. Shui Tau Tsuen and Shui Mei Tsuen were once commonly referred to as Pak Wai after that old walled village. The collective name for the two villages has remained to this day, as you see displayed on the signs of mini-buses.

At the end of the Qing dynasty, the countryside of southern China became a twilight zone of lawlessness, and incursions of bandits into Hong Kong from the Chinese borders were not infrequent. Because of a shortage of manpower to carry out policing, the traditional system of village vigilantes was maintained in the New Territories well into the 1960s. This tradition stemmed from imperial times. The volunteers were paid a small stipend by local villages, and some had uniforms though most were identified with armbands. Trained in the Chinese martial arts, they were armed with long poles and gongs as they patrolled the villages at night. In the 20th century, some vigilante groups, such as those in Kam Tin, were issued with shotguns and their offices equipped with telephones for contacting the nearest police stations.[2] During village festivals, members of the vigilante, whose training curriculum included lion dancing as a means to keep fit and agile, showed off their lion-dancing skills as they competed with other vigilante groups from neighbouring villages. The days of village vigilantes are long gone, but the relic of this paramilitary tradition can be seen in a small, dilapidated building standing inconspicuously along Kam Tin Main Road. Adorned with the fading words 'Kam Tin South Village Guard', this 1957 single-storey concrete box of a building now serves the peaceful role of a clubhouse for the elderly.

As we continued to talk, Johnny pointed at a courtyard space, now in semi-ruin, next to the Hung Shing Temple, and said,

> That's Cheung Chun Yuen ['Everlasting Spring Garden']; it's quite a famous place in our village. It was a martial arts training ground where village vigilantes used to practise fighting skills and the

> lion dance. During imperial times, it was where martial scholars trained and prepared for examinations that would qualify them as military officers. The depressions you see on the brick-paved surface of the courtyard were made by successive batches of trainees stomping on the ground as they practised.

Indeed, Shui Mei Tsuen had a glorious martial history, having produced a number of 'martial scholars' during the Qing dynasty, whose names and titles are commemorated on large timber plaques displayed in the local ancestral halls. But whatever became of the walled village of Pak Wai? We persisted with increasing curiosity, and Johnny continued his story:

> Well, it fell into disuse before I was born. I was told that during my grandfather's time, plague broke out within the village, and many of its inhabitants died. The survivors, citing bad feng-shui, abandoned the village and settled into Shui Tau Tsuen and Shui Mei Tsuen. I used to play there when I was a child, but adults in the village always told us not to go near that place. The walled village was built of strong grey bricks, exactly in the manner of Kat Hing Wai. After the war, because of shortages of materials, villagers started to dismantle the village walls and buildings for building materials. Many of the older houses in Shui Tau Tsuen and Shui Mei Tsuen were built or repaired with bricks taken from the old walled village.

In 1894, Hong Kong suffered a major outbreak of plague that killed thousands of people. The source of the plague was Canton (now Guangzhou), and the disease spread all the way down south through the New Territories to Victoria Island (now Hong Kong Island). The epidemic only came under control in 1904, and it was not declared over until 1929.[3] It is conceivable that the outbreak of plague in Pak Wai was part of this epidemic. As Johnny told us, the cannibalized remains of the walled village were eventually sold (probably in the 1970s) and what was left of it was demolished to make way for a chicken farm. 'The farm has since gone bankrupt, but its remains are still there, just north of Shui Mei Tsuen.'

Fig. 48 Cheung Chun Yuen, once a martial arts school that produced a number of martial scholars during the Qing dynasty, is now used as an ancestral hall for Shui Tau Tsuen. *(Lee Ho Yin)*

Fig. 49 The martial arts training ground behind Cheung Chun Yuen. Slight depressions on the brick-paved surface are said to have been made by martial arts students practicing on the same spots over the years. *(Lee Ho Yin)*

Fig. 50 A moat, overgrown by water-weeds, is one of the few remaining pieces of architectural evidence that Chi's Farm (an abandoned chicken farm to the north of Shui Mei Tsuen) was once a walled village. *(Lee Ho Yin)*

Fig. 51 A neglected Earth God shrine that once guarded the entrance to the demolished walled village of Pak Wai. *(Lee Ho Yin)*

Curiosity propelled us towards the site of the old walled village. We first passed a muddy stream where several water buffaloes wallowed, left to fend for themselves as they no longer served any farming purpose. Five minutes later, we came to what looked like an old farm, at the entrance to which stood two concrete posts painted with the Chinese characters that read 'Chi's Farm'. There were still visible signs of an old walled village—a neglected Earth God shrine that used to mark the entrance to the village—and remains of the surrounding moat, now almost obscured with a thick layer of water weeds. It was getting dark and the abandoned chicken farm took on an ominous appearance. Mindful of the fact that it was once a hot zone of the plague, we shuddered and quickly left.

The Rice Farmer's Story

IN SPEAKING WITH A NUMBER OF VILLAGERS, we learned that the life of a traditional farmer, being based on a seasonal cycle of agricultural activities, was uneventful and predictable. As we wandered into Shui Tau Tsuen, we stumbled upon a simple but well-kept traditional village house, hidden from the main path by the first row of village houses. We peeked into the opened door, and were startled to see a face smiling back at us. The old man had been sitting very still in the unlit living room, quietly observing us as we went snooping around outside his house. Laughing as he saw us jump, he waved at us and invited us in. Of course, he introduced himself as 'Mr. Tang' and told us that he could not remember how old he was, but most probably over 80. We asked about village life in the past, and soon he was reminiscing about his rice-planting days:

> We were able to grow two crops a year as our fields were well irrigated. Farmers farther up north near the seacoast could only manage one crop per year, as the soil in their fields was salty. We grew a variety of rice, but our most famous was *sze mew* ('silky young rice'), which fetched good prices in the Yuen Long Market. We started tilling the land with water buffaloes in early Spring, around the third lunar month, to get the fields ready for planting rice seedlings. These days, we don't grow rice

any more, and you still see some of the abandoned buffaloes wandering about.

Anyway, it was all hard work, and young people these days just have no idea how hard life was. By around the sixth lunar month, the rice was ready for harvest. It was quite a sight to see the golden rippling of the rice stalks blowing in the wind. Immediately after harvest, we went through the same routine again to prepare for the second crop, which would be ready for harvest at the end of the year, in about the tenth lunar month.

Harvesting wasn't the end of the job; there was more work to follow. We had to thresh the grain stalks, after which we had to dry the rice grains in the sun. That was a time when you saw all the rice grains laid out everywhere, in front of our houses, on the village square, on the open ground in front of the temple; just everywhere! When the grains were sufficiently dried, we gathered them and ran them through a winnowing machine to remove sand and grit. Have you seen a winnowing machine before? Come here, I'll show you.

We obediently followed the old man out of the house. He led us to a storage-shed and pulled open the thin piece of plywood that served as a flimsy door. As our eyes adjusted to the unlit interior, we saw a large wooden object that vaguely resembled a cement mixer. It was a traditional Chinese winnowing machine, which we recalled seeing at a local museum of history. He touched the dusty surface of the drum-like part of the device and started explaining enthusiastically:

This is how it works: you pour in the grains into this funnel at this end, and you turn this handle here to spin the fan blades inside to blow out the dirt. Out come the clean grains at this end, which we collected in large rattan baskets, like the ones you see stacked up in the corner.

The rice grains weren't ready to be sold at this stage. We still had to grind and pound them into polished white rice before they could be sold. My family took the easy way out—instead of doing all the work ourselves, we carried the coarse grains in

Fig. 52 Like many other senior villagers, eighty-two-year-old Mr. Tang Kiu-hing of Shui Tau Tsuen experienced a hard life of rice farming as well as the hardships of the Japanese Occupation. *(Lee Ho Yin)*

buffalo-drawn carts to Yuen Long Market, where there were shops with machines to process them.

We retained some rice grains as seeds, and we also kept some of the processed rice to eat ourselves. You know, rice planted by your own hands just tastes better! It was a good thing that we had our own farmland and we didn't have to rent fields to farm. During the Japanese Occupation period, labour costs were so cheap that we even hired people to do the farming!

After the war, Farmer Tang had had enough of farming and decided to do something else. He had always been interested in herbal medicine, and had enjoyed the times in his childhood picking herbs in the nearby hills with his mother. And so, he took up a job as an apprentice to a traditional Chinese doctor to learn the trade. In time, he practised on his own and became the resident doctor in a herbal medicine shop in Yuen Long, taking 'a ten-cent bus ride to work everyday.' Farmer Tang, who later became Doctor Tang, is a contented man. He now lives with one of his sons in a small modern house in the village, but he occasionally stops by his ancestral house just to sit in the dark and dream about old times.

The Old Village Chief's Story

TANG TIM-KAU (*DENG TIANQIU*), THE EIGHTY-FIVE-YEAR-OLD village patriarch and immediate past Village Representative of Shui Mei Tsuen, has lived in his village all his life. He has therefore witnessed the transformation of his village and the neighbouring village from the traditional past to the modern present.

We first met old Mr Tang through his eldest daughter, who was cooking in one of the few remaining traditional houses in the village. As she noticed us pausing at the doorway, she asked suspiciously what we were doing. When we explained that we were interested in her nice old building, she immediately put down her frying pan and took us to her father's house next door. It was an early 'small house', very simple and unadorned, a reinforced concrete building whose external walls were finished in old-fashioned Shanghai plaster. 'Now this is a nice house', she said. 'But we like your traditional house', we politely protested. 'No, no,' she insisted, 'there's nothing nice about that old building; it's old, and we would have torn it down if it wasn't our ancestral house!'

At this point, old Mr Tang came out from the back of the newer building. After figuring out what we were up to, he laughed out loud and pointed to a brand new small house nearby. 'That is even nicer,' he proudly declared, 'and it belongs to one of my grandsons.' At that point, we felt a little ashamed of ourselves as we realized our naïve arrogance in trying to impose our romantic notion of what village houses should look like. Like other villagers, old Mr Tang and his family did not want to be stuck in our romantic ideals, they wanted to live in modern buildings blessed with the kind of conveniences that we urbanites take for granted. As we

Fig. 53 The interior of Mr. Tang Tim-kau's old village house. *(Lee Ho Yin)*

Fig. 54 The house of Mr. Tang Tim-kau, the past Village Representative of Shui Mei Tsuen. His old house is on the right side of the photo. *(Lee Ho Yin)*

quietly swallowed our humble pie, the old man told us, in his heavily accented Cantonese, some of his village's oral history:

> Of course, there were none of the things you see today, but old-style village houses built of mud bricks and, for the wealthier villagers, clay bricks. All around the village were paddy fields in which my clansmen and I toiled. There was not even a paved path in the village, just dirt tracks that turned muddy during the rainy season. You know that bridge spanning across the [Kam Tin] river before you come into Shui Tau Tsuen? That used to be a stone bridge. When the Japanese army invaded, British troops blew it up. After the war, British soldiers came and replaced the destroyed bridge with the one you see today [which is a Bailey bridge].
>
> When my uncle died in the 1960s, I took over his position as the village head. There was no election then, the villagers simply

Fig. 55 A group of elderly village women playing cards and relaxing under the shade of a tree in Shui Tau Tsuen's village square. *(Lee Ho Yin)*

Fig. 56 The Bailey bridge built by the British military after World War II to replace the one blown up during the war to slow Japanese advances. This steel bridge is still in use today. *(Information Services Department, Hong Kong)*

sent a letter to the District Office informing the officer of my nomination, and that was it. I was responsible for all the paved paths in the village. The government helped by providing cement and building materials, which I had to ask for in writing. It was us, the villagers, who laid the paths with our own hands.

At this point, he pointed at a fading colour photograph hanging at the far end of the sitting room. We were surprised. It was a picture of him shaking hands with HRH Prince Charles! What happened here, we queried. Oh, he said in his usual calm voice, there's a good story there, and he told us this remarkable tale:

> There were still no roads leading to the village in the '70s. I had written many times to the District Office for help but none came. The reason given was that our village was too small to justify a proper road. I wasn't too happy about that! Then the Prince was due to visit Hong Kong [in 1979 to inaugurate the

newly completed Prince of Wales Building—now renamed Chinese People's Liberation Army Forces Hong Kong Building], and he was interested in seeing some old villages. Our village, being famously old, was chosen. Some government people came to see me—you see, they had to ask my permission first before the Prince could visit. I knew the opportunity had come.

As he paused briefly to sip his tea, we detected a mischievous twinkle in his eyes. He continued his story:

I told them 'No', the prince would not be allowed to come to our village. They were shocked, as they did not expect me to say no! They asked why, and I told them that I couldn't possibly invite the prince into our village without a properly paved road. They got the message, and a few days later, the District Office sent a surveyor with a letter promising to have the road built.

Fig. 57 The road leading to Shui Mei Tsuen's village committee office. There was no paved road leading to the village until 1979, when HRH Prince Charles decided to visit this historical village. *(Lee Ho Yin)*

Within days, workmen and machines turned up and the road for which I had petitioned the government for years was quickly completed. So, I really had the prince to thank for the nice road!

At the end of this wonderful story, we felt united in spirit with old Mr. Tang, who beamed at us with a satisfied smile. Then Mr. Tang sighed, and with a mild tinge of bitterness, he added,

I've worked so hard for this village, and I ask for nothing in return. The government has shown no appreciation for my effort. Nothing! Not even a simple 'thank you'. I'm old now, and my eldest son has taken over my place as the village head. I hope he can do better.

We struggled to come up with the appropriate consoling words, but our minds were blank. It was time for us to leave, we concluded, and that was all we could do. Months later, when we returned to visit old Mr. Tang, he showed us into his house again, and immediately pointed at a framed document on the wall. It was an official certificate from the government, which read:

> This is in special recognition
> of the services rendered
> to the people of Hong Kong
> by
>
> Mr. TANG Tim-kau
>
> as Village Representative
> of Shui Mei Tsuen,
> Kam Tin
> for the period
> 1967–1999
>
> Date: 4 May 1999
>
> (Signed) Mrs. Shelley Lau
> Director of Home Affairs

Fig. 58 Until the advent of 'Spanish-style villas' brought about by the Small House Policy, the physical environment of Shui Tau Tsuen and Shui Mei Tsuen was full of traditional village buildings built of Chinese grey bricks, and the internal streets were partially paved with granite slabs. This photograph was taken in 1976. *(Information Services Department, Hong Kong)*

Notes

[1] The figures check out, as the official figures (1996 census) for the combined registered population of Shui Tau Tsuen, Shui Mei Tsuen, and the nearby tiny village of Kam Hing are 1,071. These include people of both sexes in 343 households.
[2] See: Fung 1996, 13; Yau 1992, 66.
[3] See: Siu 1989, 17.

Bibliography

Antiquities and Monuments Office, *Yi Tai Study Hall* [pamphlet], Hong Kong: Leisure and Cultural Services Department, n. d.

Baker, Hugh D. R., 'The Five Great Clans of the New Territories', *Journal of the Hong Kong Branch of the Royal Asiatic Society*, Vol. 6 (1966), 25–47.

Bruce, Philip, *Second to None: The Story of the Hong Kong Volunteers*, Hong Kong: Oxford University Press, 1991.

Buddle, Cliff, 'Ancestral Voting "a Colonial Leftover" ', *South China Morning Post*, 10 March 1999, 6.

Chan, Quinton, 'Two Heads Better Than One?', *Sunday Morning Post*, 1 April 2001, 11.

Endacott, G. B., *A History of Hong Kong*, rev. ed., Hong Kong: Oxford University Press, 1973.

Faure, David, 'The Tangs of Kam Tin—A Hypothesis on the Rise of a Gentry Family', in *From Village to City: Studies in the Traditional Roots of Hong Kong Society*, ed. David Faure, James Hayes, and Alan Birch, 24–42, Hong Kong: Centre of Asian Studies, The University of Hong Kong, 1984.

Freedman, Maurice, 'A Report on Social Research in the New Territories of Hong Kong, 1963', *Journal of the Hong Kong Branch of the Royal Asiatic Society*, Vol. 16 (1976), 191–261.

Fung, C. M., *Yuen Long Historical Relics and Monuments*, Hong Kong: Yuen Long District Board, 1996.

Hayes, James, 'The Nature of Village Life', in *From Village to City: Studies in the Traditional Roots of Hong Kong Society*, ed. David Faure, James Hayes, and Alan Birch, 55–72, Hong Kong: Centre of Asian Studies, The University of Hong Kong, 1984.

Ho, Joyce W. Y. and C. O. Yau; edited by Tom K. C. Ming (何惠儀、游子安撰，明基全編),《教不倦：新界傳統教育的蛻變》*From Study Hall to Village School* (a bilingual publication), Hong Kong: The Regional Council, 1996.

Hong Kong Government, *Annual Report on Hong Kong for the Year 1946*, Hong Kong: Government of Hong Kong, 1947.

Hong Kong Government, *A Gazetteer of Place Names in Hong Kong, Kowloon and the New Territories*, Hong Kong: Government Printer, 1960.

Kamm, Thomas J., 'Field Notes on the Social History and Fung-shui of Kam Tin', *Journal of the Hong Kong Branch of the Royal Asiatic Society*, Vol. 17 (1978), 202–216.

Lai, Chloe, 'Daughters Inherited Community Mission', *Sunday Morning Post*, 18 July 1999, 3.

Lau, N. K., 'One Village, Two Chiefs', *South China Morning Post*, Analysis, 24 April 2001, 22.

Lau, Y. W. (劉潤和),《新界簡史》[A brief history of the New Territories], Hong Kong: Joint Publishing (H.K) Co., Ltd., 1999.

Lee, M. K., 'The Evolution of the Heung Yee Kuk as a Political Institution', in *From Village to City: Studies in the Traditional Roots of Hong Kong Society*, ed. David Faure, James Hayes, and Alan Birch, 164–177, Hong Kong: Centre of Asian Studies, The University of Hong Kong, 1984.

Lee, Sherry, 'A Wall of Contention', *South China Morning Post*, Focus Section, 26 February 2001, 1.

Leung, K. H. (梁廣漢),《香港前代古跡述略》[A profile of historic relics in the early stage of Hong Kong], Hong Kong: Hok Jun Books (學津書店), 1980.

Li, Angela, 'Way Open for more Challenges to Indigenous Villagers' Special Rights', *Sunday Morning Post*, 14 March 1999, 2.

Liu C. K. (劉存寬),《租借新界》[Lease of the New Territories], Hong Kong: Joint Publishing (H.K.) Co., Ltd., 1995.

Lockhart, J. H. Stewart, 'Extracts from the Lockhart Report on the New Territory, 8 October, 1898, from Great Britain', published on the Website: http://hkuhist2.hku.hk/firstyear/Sinn/sinnE04-2.htm, extracted from Colonial Office Document (Hong Kong), CO 129/289, 8 Oct. 1898.

_____, 'Report on the New Territory at Hong Kong' (report presented to the Houses of Parliament, Nov. 1900), London: Her Majesty's Stationery Office, 1900.

Loh, Christine K. W., 'Inheritance Rights of Indigenous Women of the New Territories', published in the Citizens Party website: http://www.citizensparty.org/law/inherit.html, Hong Kong: Citizens Party, 2001.

Mo, P. Y., 'Villagers Win Election Battle', *South China Morning Post*, 23 December 2000, 1.

Ng, K. C., 'Kuk's Patriarchy Makes Last Stand', *South China Morning Post*, 18 April 2001, 14.

Ng, Peter, Y. L., *New Peace County: A Chinese Gazetteer of the Hong Kong Region*, Hong Kong: Hong Kong University Press, 1983.

Sinclair, Kevin, 'The Lucrative Lie Built on "Native Son" Foundations', *Sunday Morning Post*, 19 September 1999, 2.

_____, 'Rotten Roots of Village Polls', *South China Morning Post*, 7 February 2001, 13.

_____, 'NT's Old Village System Rotten to the Core', *South China Morning Post*, 23 October 2000, 17.

Siu, Anthony K. K. (蕭國健),《香港史地探索文集》[A compendium of history of places in Hong Kong], Hong Kong: Hin Chiu Institute, 1989.

_____,《香港新界家族發展》[The development of clans in the New Territories, Hong Kong], Hong Kong: Hin Chiu Institute, 1990.

Sung, H. P., 'Legends and Stories of the New Territories: Kam Tin', *Journal of the Hong Kong Branch of the Royal Asiatic Society*, Vol. 13 (1973), 111–129.

_____, 'Legends and Stories of the New Territories: Kam Tin', *Journal of the Hong Kong Branch of the Royal Asiatic Society*, Vol. 14 (1974), 160–185.

_____, 'Legends and Stories of the New Territories: Kam Tin', *Journal of the Hong Kong Branch of the Royal Asiatic Society*, Vol. 17 (1978), 202–214.

U. K. Colonial Office Records, Series CO 129/289: *Lockhart Report on the New Territories, 8 October, 1898, from Great Britain*, October 1898.

Welsh, Frank, *A History of Hong Kong*, London: HarperCollins Publishers, 1993.

Wesley-Smith, Peter, 'The Kam Tin Gates', *Journal of the Hong Kong Branch of the Royal Asiatic Society*, Vol. 13 (1973), 40–44.
Wordie, Jason, 'When Hong Kong was New Peace County', *Sunday Morning Post*, 15 April 2001, 12.
Yau, T. (邱東),《新界風物与民情》[Scenes and lives of the New Territories], Hong Kong: Joint Publishing (H.K.) Co., Ltd., 1992.

Index

Agricultural economy of the New Territories 79–80

Bailey bridge *123 (Fig. 56)*
Basic Law 89
Battle of Kam Tin 66, 67, 69–70
Blake, Sir Henry 62, 67, *67 (Fig. 14)*, 71, 72

Chamberlain, Joseph 62
Cheung Chun Yuen 113, *115 (Fig. 48, Fig. 49)*, Plate 5, Plate 6
Court of Final Appeal 94, 95
Chou Wong Yi Kung Shue Yuen ('Study Hall of the Two Lords Zhou and Wang') *2 (Fig. 1)*, 55
Coastal Evacuation Order 2 (caption, Fig. 1), 46, 48–51, 55

Dongguan 33, 35, 39, 41, 43, 49, 58 (n. 36), 68

Emperors
    Chenghua (Ming dynasty) 55
    Gaozong (Southern Song dynasty) 35, 36, 38, 39, 40
    Guangwu (Han dynasty) 29
    Guangxu (Qing dynasty) 66
    Guangzong (Southern Song dynasty) 37, 40
    Huang Ti (mythical dynasty) 29
    Huizong (Northern Song dynasty) 36
    Kangxi (Qing dynasty) 46, 49, 55
    Qinzong (Northern Song dynasty) 36
    Pingti (Western Han dynasty) 57 (n. 10)
    Shunzhi (Qing dynasty) 48
    Zuding (Shang dynasty) 29

Fame, H.M.S. 68
Feng shui 31, 32, 41, 106, 110, 114

Genghis Khan 43
Gurkha soldiers 95, 96, *96* (caption, Fig. 28)

Ha Tsuen 35
Hakkas 53, 54, 59 (n. 48)
Heung Yee Kuk 86, 87, 89, 95
Hong Kong Regiment 68, 71, 77 (n. 18)
Hong Kong Volunteers *60 (Fig. 12)*, 68, *70 (Fig. 16)*, 77 (n. 18)
Hung Shing Temple 78 (caption, Fig. 18), 99 (caption, Fig. 34), 100, *103 (Fig. 39)*, 113, Plate 9, Plate 16

Indigenous villagers 20, 88, 94, 95

Japanese Occupation of Hong Kong 66, 74, 76, 119 (caption, Fig. 52)

Kam Tin
    Chan Tin 27
    Origins of name 28, 44
    Shum Lei 27, 28
    Shum Lei Tin 28
    Shum Tin 28, 37, 38, 43
    Tang villages 28, 56 (n. 5)
    Topography 27–28
    Walled villages
        Kam Hing Wai 33, 55
        Kam Shui Wai 33
        Kat Hing Wai *51 (Fig. 11a)*, 55, 63, *65 (Fig. 13)*, 66, 67 (caption, Fig. 14), 71, 72, 73, 73 (caption, Fig. 17), 77 (n. 20), 103 (caption, Fig. 41), 114, Plate 1
        Nam Wai 33, 34, 35
        Pak Wai 33, 34, 35, 113, 114, *116* (Fig. 51)
        Tai Hong Wai 46, *47 (Fig.10)*, *52 (Fig. 11b)*, 55, 64 (caption, Fig. 13), 67 (caption, Fig., 14), 71, 72, 96, *96 (Fig. 28)*
        Wing Long Wai *52 (Fig. 11c)*, 55

Kam Tin River *34 (Fig. 7)*, 34, 35, 38, 63
Korean War 80
Kwai Kok Shan 30, 57 (n. 16)

Lam Tsuen Valley 69
Lease of New Territories 20, 55, 61, 64
Land ownership 32, 32 (caption, Fig. 6), 84, 86
Lee Man-wing 45, 46
Lockhart, James Haldane Stewart 62, 63, 64, 68, 69, *69 (Fig. 15)*, 71
Lockhart Report (1898) 62
Lockhart's report to the House of Parliament (1900) 64, 72
Lord Salisbury 61, 76 (n. 1)
Lung Yeuk Tau 35, 59 (n. 46), 64 (caption, Fig. 13)

Maxim gun *60 (Fig. 12)*, 63–64, 68
May, Henry 68

Nantou 43, 54, 68
Nepalese in Hong Kong 95, 96, *96 (Fig. 28)*
New Towns 86, 105

Opium Wars 55, 56

People's Liberation Army 95, 124
Ping Shan 35, 72
Plague 114, 117
Prince Charles, HRH 123, 124, 124 (caption, Fig. 57)
Puntis 54

Rice cultivation 44, 79–80, 117–119
Robinson, Sir William 67
Royal Marines 63

San On Gazetteer 30, 35, 49, 56 (n. 1), *Plate 3*
Sex Discrimination Ordinance 89, 95
Shek Kong Airfield 28, 70, 75, 95
Shek Tau Wai 69, 70
Shenzhen 43, 66, 68
Sheung Tsuen 69, 70, 71
Small House Policy 83, 84 (caption, Fig. 21), 87–91, 105, 106 (n. 6, n. 7), 109
Stubbs, Sir Reginald 72, 73, *73 (Fig. 17)*, 74

Tai Po 56 (n. 2), 67, 68, 71, 77 (n. 27)
Tang Ching Lok Ancestral Hall *92 (Fig. 25)*, *98 (Fig. 31)*, *99 (Fig. 34)*, 104, *Plate 8*
Tang clan, prominent ancestors
   Earliest traceable ancestor Tang Yue 29, 57 (n. 10)
   First ancestor Tang Man (Tang Tak-yueng) 29
   'Five Yuens' (sons of Tang Kwai and Tang Sui) 35
   Tang Fu (Tang Fu-hip) 29, 30, 31, 32, 33, 35, 37, 56 (n. 1), 57 (n. 17)
      His two sons Po and Yeung 33
   Tang Gai-yue 55
   Tang Hon-fat 29, 32
   Tang Kwai 33, 35
   Tang Man-wai 46, 54, 59 (n. 38, n. 39)
   Tang Pak-kau 72
   Tang Sui 33
   Tang Wai-kap (Tang Tsz-ming) 35, 36, 37, 40
      His four sons Lam, Gei, Wai and Chi 37, 40
   Tang Yuen-fan 43, 44
   Tang Yuen-leung 35, 36, 37, 38

Tang resistance to British rule 66–70, 88
Tang villagers, contemporary
   Tang, Johnny 34, 81, 112–114, 112 (caption, Fig. 47)
   Tang Kiu-hing *119 (Fig. 52)*
   Tang Po-luk 34
   Tang Tim-kau 75, 81, 96, 104, 105, *108 (Fig. 43)*, 120, 121 (captions, Fig. 53, Fig. 54), 122–125
Tanka 56 (n. 1)
Tartars 36, 37
Tsuen Wan 32, 56 (n. 2)

Village Representatives 76, 93, 94, 95, 112, 125
Village vigilantes 100, 113

Wang Lairen, Governor 2 (caption, Fig. 1), 49, 50, 55
West Rail Project 16, 17, 21 (caption, Fig. 2), 22, 105, 106, 107 (n. 18)
Women's rights 91, 93
Wong Ku 37, 38, 39, 40, 41, 42, 42 (caption, Fig. 8), 93

Xin'an county 43, 44, 45, 48, 51, 53, 54, 55, 57 (n. 12), 58 (n. 36), 64

Yi Tai Study Hall *31 (Fig. 5)*
Yuen Long 14, 32, 54, 56 (n. 2), 70, 77 (n. 27), 119

Zheng Chenggong (Koxinga) 48, 49
Zhou Youde, Viceroy 2 (caption, Fig. 1), 50, 55

About the Authors

DR. LEE HO YIN, a Hong Kong-born Cantonese who grew up in Singapore, has been living and working in Hong Kong since his return to his birthplace in 1992. Trained as an architect, he obtained his doctoral degree with a thesis on the socio-cultural aspect of the traditional Malay houseform, part of which will be published in a chapter of a book to be published by Oxford University Press. Ho Yin is currently an honorary assistant professor and a research fellow in the University of Hong Kong's postgraduate Architectural Conservation Programme. He occasionally collaborates with Lynne, the co-author of this book, as conservation consultant for local and regional governments. An avid photographer since his secondary school days, when he served as the president of his school's photographic society, he employs his photography in public lectures to help promote awareness of Hong Kong's built heritage.

Ken Chung

DR. LYNNE D. DISTEFANO, a Canadian who was born and raised in upstate New York, came to Hong Kong in 1997 and has lived and worked there since. Trained as an historian, she served for twenty-one years as an associate professor at Brescia College, the University of Western Ontario, and later for seven years as Chief Curator at Museum London in Ontario, Canada. In 1998, Lynne joined the Department of Architecture at the University of Hong Kong, where she currently serves as Honorary Associate Professor and Curriculum Coordinator for the postgraduate Architectural

Conservation Programme. In 2001, she was invited by the Office of the UNESCO Regional Advisor for Culture in Asia and the Pacific to participate as an expert in the conference/workshop *Culture Heritage Management & Tourism* in Lijiang, China. She recently curated a major exhibition for Museum London, *The Ontario Cottage*, about a vernacular houseform found throughout the British Empire during the 19th century.

Book Design by Lea & Ink Design

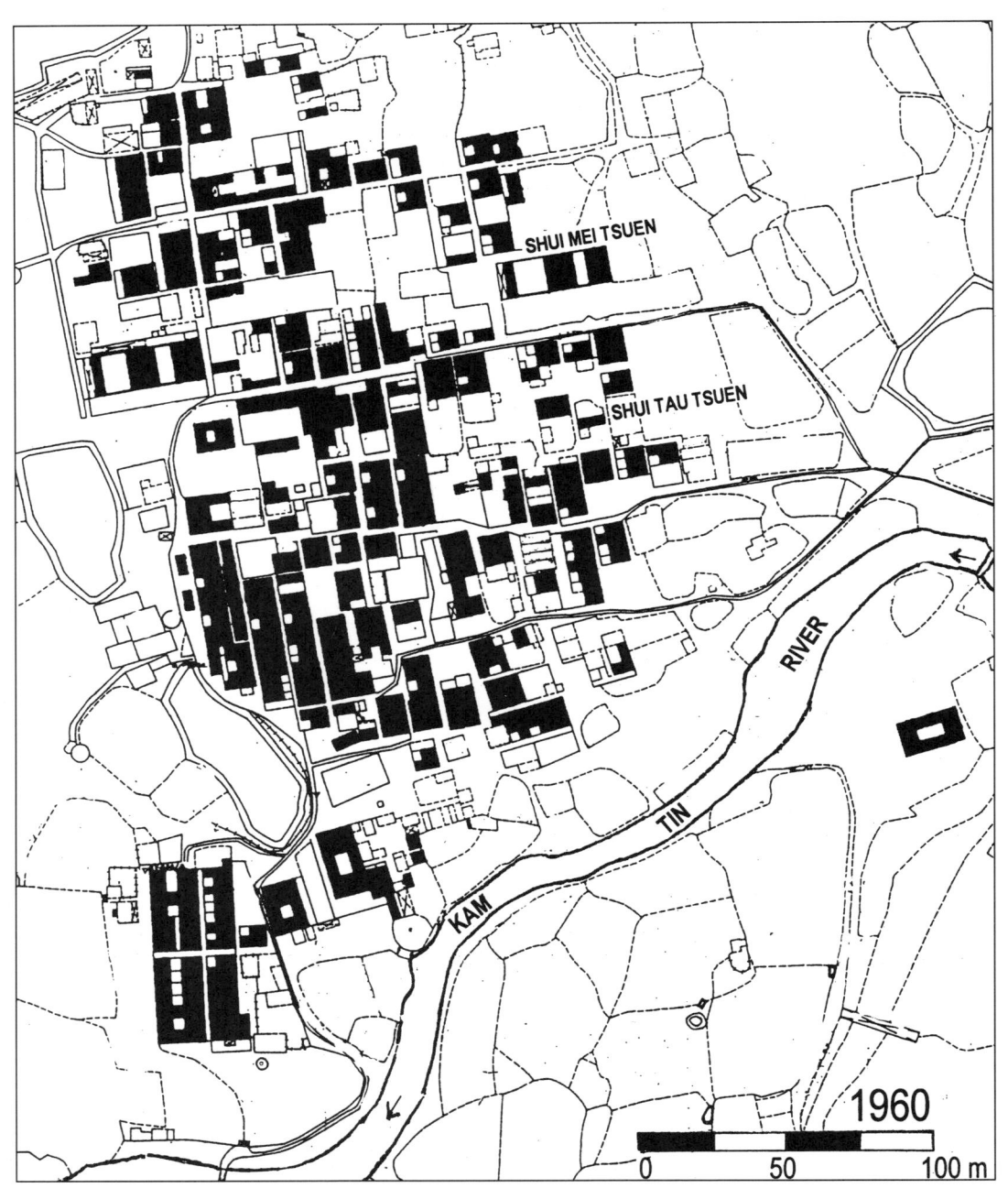